Add your opinion to our next book

Fill out a survey

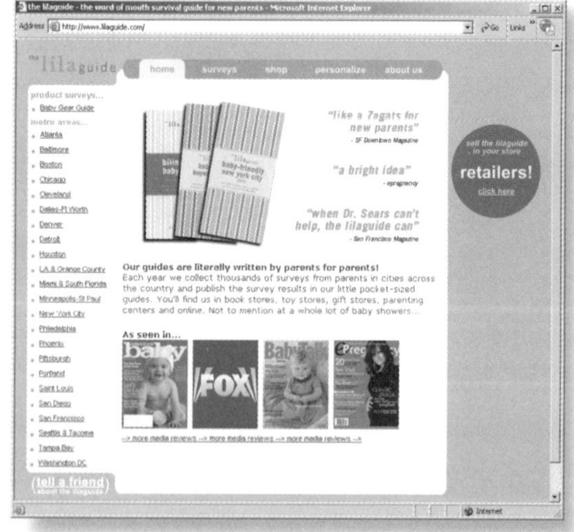

visit www.lilaguide.com

the lila guide

by PARENTS *for* PARENTS

baby-friendly baltimore area

NEW PARENT SURVIVAL GUIDE TO SHOPPING, ACTIVITIES, RESTAURANTS AND MORE...

1ST EDITION

LOCAL EDITOR: LIZ BAER

PUBLISHED BY THE LILAGUIDE/OAM SOLUTIONS, INC.
SAN FRANCISCO, CA   WWW.LILAGUIDE.COM

Published by:
OAM Solutions, Inc.
139 Saturn Street
San Francisco, CA 94114, USA
415.252.1300
orders@lilaguide.com
www.lilaguide.com

ISBN. 1-932847-12-X
First Printing: 2005
Printed in the USA

This book is designed to share parents' opinions regarding baby-related products, services and activities. It is sold with the understanding that the information contained in the book does not represent the publisher's opinion or recommendations.
The reviews contained in this guide are based on public opinion surveys and are therefore subjective in nature. The publisher shall have neither liability nor responsibility to any person or entity with respect to any loss or damage caused, or alleged to have been caused, directly or indirectly, by the information contained in this book.

If you do not wish to be bound by the above, you may return this book to the publisher for a full refund.

table of contents

No, for the last time, the baby does not come with a handbook. And even if there were a handbook, you wouldn't read it. You'd fill out the warranty card, throw out the box, and start playing right away. Until a few hours passed and you were hit with the epiphany of, "Gee whiz honey, what in the wide, wide world of childcare are we doing here?"

Relax. We had that panicked thought when we had our daughter Delilah. And so did **all the parents** we talked to when they had their children. And while we all knew there was no handbook, there was, we found, a whole lot of **word-of-mouth information**. Everyone we talked to had some bit of child rearing advice about what baby gear store is the most helpful. Some **nugget of parenting wisdom** about which restaurant tolerates strained carrots on the floor. It all really seemed to help. Someone, we thought, should write this down.

And that's when, please pardon the pun, the lilaguide was born. The book you're now holding is a guide **written by local parents for local parents**. It's what happens when someone actually does write it down (and organizes it, calculates it, and presents it in an easy-to-use format).

Nearly 2,300 surveys have produced this first edition of **the lilaguide: Baby-Friendly Baltimore Area**. It provides a truly unique insider's view of over 500 "parent-friendly" stores, activities, restaurants, and service providers that are about to become a very big part of your life. And while this guide won't tell you how to change a diaper or how to get by on little or no sleep (that's what grandparents are for), it will tell you what other **local parents have learned** about the amazing things your city and neighborhood have to offer.

As you peruse these reviews, please remember that this guide is **not intended to be a comprehensive directory** since it does not contain every baby store or activity in the area. Rather, it is intended to provide a short-list of places that your neighbors and friends **deemed exciting and noteworthy**. If a place or business is not listed, it simply means that nobody (or not enough people) rated or submitted information about it to us. **Please let us know** about your favorite parent and baby-friendly businesses and service providers by participating in our online survey at **www.lilaguide.com**. We always want your opinions!

So there you have it. Now go make some phone calls, clean up the house, take a nap, or do something on your list before the baby arrives.

Enjoy!

Oli & Elysa

Oli Mittermaier & Elysa Marco, MD

PS

We love getting feedback (good and bad) so don't be bashful. Email us at **lila@lilaguide.com** with your thoughts, comments and suggestions. We'll be sure to try to include them in next year's edition!

We'd like to take a moment to offer a heart-felt thank you to all the **parents who participated in our survey** and took the time to share their thoughts and opinions. Without your participation, we would never have been able to create this unique guide.

Thanks also to **Amy Fallavena** for helping identify additional hot tot spots in Baltimore, and **Lisa Barnes**, **Nora Borowsky**, **Todd Cooper**, **Amy Iannone**, **Katy Jacobson**, **Felicity John Odell**, **Shira Johnson**, **Kasia Kappes**, **Jen Krug**, **Dana Kulvin**, **Deborah Schneider**, **Kevin Schwall**, **April Stewart**, and **Nina Thompson** for their tireless editorial eyes; **Satoko Furuta** and **Paul D. Smith** for their beautiful sense of design, and **Lane Foard** for making the words yell.

Special thanks to **Paul D. Smith**, **Ken Miles**, and **Ali Wing** for their consistent support and overall encouragement in all things lilaguide, and of course **our parents** for their unconditional support in this and all our other endeavors.

And last, but certainly not least, thanks to **little Delilah** for inspiring us to embark on this challenging, yet incredibly fulfilling project.

disclaimer

This book is designed to share parents' opinions regarding baby-related products, services and activities. It is sold with the understanding that the information contained in the book **does not represent the publisher's opinion** or recommendations.

The reviews contained in this guide are based on **public opinion surveys** and are therefore subjective in nature. The publisher shall have neither liability nor responsibility to any person or entity with respect to any loss or damage caused, or alleged to have been caused, directly or indirectly, by the information contained in this book.

ratings

Most listings have stars and numbers as part of their write-up. These symbols mean the following:

❺ / ★★★★★	extraordinary
❹ / ★★★★☆	very good
❸ / ★★★☆☆	good
❷ / ★★☆☆☆	fair
❶ / ★☆☆☆☆	poor
✓	available
✗	not available/relevant

If a ★ is listed instead of ★, it means that the rating is less reliable because a small number of parents surveyed the listing. Furthermore, if a listing has **no stars** or **criteria ratings**, it means that although the listing was rated, the number of surveys submitted was so low that we did not feel it justified an actual rating.

quotes & reviews

The quotes/reviews are taken directly from surveys submitted to us via our web site (**www.lilaguide.com**). Other than spelling and minor grammatical changes, they come to you as they came to us. Quotes were selected based on how well they appeared to represent the collective opinions of the surveys submitted.

fact checking

We have contacted all of the businesses listed to verify their address and phone number, as well as to inquire about their hours, class schedules and web site information. Since some of this information may change after this guide has been printed, we appreciate you letting us know of any errors by notifying us via email at **lila@lilaguide.com**.

baby basics & accessories

Baltimore City

"lila picks"

★Bellini

★Bratt Décor

★Eieio

★IKEA

★Pied Piper

★Raw Sugar

★Red Canoe

Amuse

"...a unique toy and gift store... lots of unusual and educational toys... worth visiting... you may be able to get things cheaper elsewhere, but the family who owns this business really knows their stuff... a treasure chest of fabulous toys... gift wrapping available just to make your life that much easier..."

Furniture, Bedding & Decor	✗	$$$	Prices
Gear & Equipment	✗	❹	Product availability
Nursing & Feeding	✗	❹	Staff knowledge
Safety & Babycare	✗	❹	Customer service
Clothing, Shoes & Accessories	✗	❹	Decor
Books, Toys & Entertainment	✓		

BALTIMORE—1623 THAMES ST (AT S BOND ST); 410.342.5000; DAILY 10-9; PARKING LOT

April Cornell

"...beautiful, classic dresses and accessories for special occasions... I love the matching 'mommy and me' outfits... lots of fun knickknacks for sale... great selection of baby wear on their web site... rest assured your baby won't look like every other child in these adorable outfits... very frilly and girlie—beautiful..."

Furniture, Bedding & Decor	✗	$$$	Prices
Gear & Equipment	✗	❸	Product availability
Nursing & Feeding	✗	❹	Staff knowledge
Safety & Babycare	✗	❹	Customer service
Clothing, Shoes & Accessories	✓	❹	Decor
Books, Toys & Entertainment	✗		

WWW.APRILCORNELL.COM

BALTIMORE—200 E PRATT ST (AT THE GALLERY AT HARBOR PLACE); 410.234.0050; M-SA 10-9, SU 11-7

Baby Depot At Burlington Coat Factory

"...a large, 'super store' layout with a ton of baby gear... wide aisles, packed shelves, barely existent customer service and awesome prices... everything from bottles, car seats and strollers to gliders, cribs and clothes... I always find something worth getting... a little disorganized and hard to locate items you're looking for... the staff is not always

knowledgeable about their merchandise... return policy is store credit only... ”

Furniture, Bedding & Decor ✓	$$ Prices
Gear & Equipment ✓	❸ Product availability
Nursing & Feeding ✓	❸ Staff knowledge
Safety & Babycare ✓	❸ Customer service
Clothing, Shoes & Accessories ✓	❸ Decor
Books, Toys & Entertainment ✓	

WWW.BABYDEPOT.COM

BALTIMORE—1955 E JOPPA RD (AT PERRING PKWY); 410.665.1390; M-SA 10-9:30, SU 11-6

BALTIMORE—6500 REISTERSTOWN RD (AT REISTERTOWN PLAZA); 410.764.3338; M-SA 10-9, SU 12-6; MALL PARKING

BALTIMORE—6901 SECURITY BLVD (AT BELMONT AVE); 410.265.1508; M-SA 10-9:30, SU 11-6; PARKING LOT

BabyGap/GapKids

“*...colorful baby and toddler clothing in clean, well-lit stores... great return policy... it's the Gap, so you know what you're getting—colorful, cute and well-made clothing... best place for baby hats... prices are reasonable especially since there's always a sale of some sort going on... sales, sales, sales—frequent and fantastic... everything I'm looking for in infant clothing—snap crotches, snaps up the front, all natural fabrics and great styling... fun seasonal selections—a great place to shop for gifts as well as for your own kids... although it can get busy, staff generally seem accommodating and helpful...* ”

Furniture, Bedding & Decor ✗	$$$ Prices
Gear & Equipment ✗	❹ Product availability
Nursing & Feeding ✗	❹ Staff knowledge
Safety & Babycare ✗	❹ Customer service
Clothing, Shoes & Accessories ✓	❹ Decor
Books, Toys & Entertainment ✗	

WWW.GAP.COM

BALTIMORE—200 E PRATT ST (AT SOUTH ST); 410.332.4143; M-SA 10-9 SU 11-7

Barston's Child's Play

“*...the ultimate toy store for kids of all ages... Gund Blankets to board games and arts and crafts... great place to find unusual gifts... staff made super gift suggestions based on age and sex of my child... helpful and friendly...* ”

Furniture, Bedding & Decor ✓	$$$ Prices
Gear & Equipment ✗	❺ Product availability
Nursing & Feeding ✗	❹ Staff knowledge
Safety & Babycare ✗	❹ Customer service
Clothing, Shoes & Accessories ✗	❸ Decor
Books, Toys & Entertainment ✓	

WWW.BARSTONSCHILDSPLAY.COM

BALTIMORE—THE VILLAGE OF CROSS KEYS (AT COLDSPRING LN); 410.435.0804; M-W F-SA 10-6, TH 10-8, SU 12-4; PARKING LOT

Bellini

★★★★★

“*...high-end furniture for a gorgeous nursery... if you're looking for the kind of furniture you see in magazines then this is the place to go... excellent quality... yes, it's pricey, but the quality is impeccable... free delivery and setup... their furniture is built to withstand the abuse my tots dish out... they sell very unique merchandise, ranging from cribs to bedding and even some clothes... our nursery design was inspired by their store decor... I wish they had more frequent sales...* ”

Furniture, Bedding & Decor ✓	$$$$ Prices
Gear & Equipment ✗	❹ Product availability

Nursing & Feeding .... ✗ ❹ .... Staff knowledge
Safety & Babycare .... ✗ ❹ ....Customer service
Clothing, Shoes & Accessories .... ✗ ❹ .... Decor
Books, Toys & Entertainment .... ✓

WWW.BELLINI.COM

BALTIMORE—1809 REISTERTOWN RD (AT WOODHOLME SHOPPING CTR); 410.486.9646; M-SA 10-6; PARKING LOT

Bratt Decor ★★★★★

"...great place for nursery design ideas... very upscale nursery and bedroom furnishings... lots of unique baby furniture and accessories... the kind of furniture you see in magazine ads—precious... a great place to find unusual decor accessories for your baby's nursery..."

Furniture, Bedding & Decor .... ✓ $$$$ .... Prices
Gear & Equipment .... ✗ ❹ ....Product availability
Nursing & Feeding .... ✗ ❹ .... Staff knowledge
Safety & Babycare .... ✗ ❹ ....Customer service
Clothing, Shoes & Accessories .... ✗ ❺ .... Decor
Books, Toys & Entertainment .... ✗

WWW.BRATTDECOR.COM

BALTIMORE—544 E BELVEDERE AVE (AT YORK AVE); 410.464.9400; M-TH 10-6, F-SA 10-7, SU 12-5; FREE PARKING

Children's Place, The ★★★½☆

"...great bargains on cute clothing... shoes, socks, swimsuits, sunglasses and everything in between... lots of '3 for $20' type deals on sleepers, pants and mix-and-match separates... so much more affordable than the other 'big chains'... don't expect the most unique stuff here, but it wears and washes well... cheap clothing for cheap prices... you can leave the store with bags full of clothes without putting a huge dent in your wallet..."

Furniture, Bedding & Decor .... ✗ $$ .... Prices
Gear & Equipment .... ✗ ❹ ....Product availability
Nursing & Feeding .... ✗ ❹ .... Staff knowledge
Safety & Babycare .... ✗ ❹ ....Customer service
Clothing, Shoes & Accessories ...... ✓ ❹ .... Decor
Books, Toys & Entertainment .... ✓

WWW.CHILDRENSPLACE.COM

BALTIMORE—8200 PERRY HALL BLVD (AT WHITE MARSH MALL); 410.931.7192; M-SA 9:30-10, SU 10-7; FREE PARKING

Costco ★★★½☆

"...dependable place for bulk diapers, wipes and formula at discount prices... clothing selection is very hit-or-miss... avoid shopping there during nights and weekends if possible, because parking and checkout lines are brutal... they don't have a huge selection of brands, but the brands they do have are almost always in stock and at a great price... lowest prices around for diapers and formula... kid's clothing tends to be picked through, but it's worth looking for great deals on name-brand items like Carter's..."

Furniture, Bedding & Decor .... ✓ $$ .... Prices
Gear & Equipment .... ✓ ❸ ....Product availability
Nursing & Feeding .... ✓ ❸ .... Staff knowledge
Safety & Babycare .... ✓ ❸ ....Customer service
Clothing, Shoes & Accessories ...... ✓ ❷ .... Decor
Books, Toys & Entertainment .... ✓

WWW.COSTCO.COM

BALTIMORE—9919 PULASKI HWY (OFF RT 95); 410.574.7563; M-F 11-8:30, SA 9:30-6, SU 10-6

Dollar General

"...on the spot entertainers for your kids when you are on the go... surprisingly this store carries all the baby gear you need—clothes, diapers and a whole lot more... for a dollar store you get a great selection of items, even some brand-names... prices are good if you can overlook the shoddy interior..."

Furniture, Bedding & Decor .... ✗
Gear & Equipment .... ✗
Nursing & Feeding .... ✗
Safety & Babycare .... ✓
Clothing, Shoes & Accessories .... ✓
Books, Toys & Entertainment .... ✓

$ .... Prices
❸ .... Product availability
❸ .... Staff knowledge
❸ .... Customer service
❸ .... Decor

WWW.DOLLARGENERAL.COM

BALTIMORE—5405 BALTIMORE NATIONAL PIKE (AT COLERIDGE RD); 410.869.1406; M-SA 9-8, SU 10-6:30

Eclectic Elements

Furniture, Bedding & Decor .... ✓
Nursing & Feeding .... ✗
Clothing, Shoes & Accessories .... ✓

✗ .... Gear & Equipment
✗ .... Safety & Babycare
✗ .... Books, Toys & Entertainment

WWW.ECLECTICELEMENTSONLINE.COM

BALTIMORE—813 S BROADWAY (AT LANCASTER ST); 410.675.5105

Eieio

"...a truly excellent consignment shop with clean, high-quality clothes that rotate by season, so you can shop often... it's so adorable that you want to buy everything... secondhand items in a boutique setting... great place with inexpensive and cool baby gear... brand-names and high-ticket items like winter coats and party dresses... the owner is wonderful and always smiling..."

Furniture, Bedding & Decor .... ✗
Gear & Equipment .... ✓
Nursing & Feeding .... ✗
Safety & Babycare .... ✗
Clothing, Shoes & Accessories .... ✓
Books, Toys & Entertainment .... ✗

$$$ .... Prices
❹ .... Product availability
❹ .... Staff knowledge
❺ .... Customer service
❹ .... Decor

WWW.CLUCKCLUCKHERE.COM

BALTIMORE—3616 FALLS RD (AT W 36TH ST); 410.889.2299; T-SA 10-6

Franklin Square Hospital Gift Shop

"...small with a limited selection... great if you are at the hospital, but I wouldn't make a special trip to this little hospital store..."

Furniture, Bedding & Decor .... ✗
Gear & Equipment .... ✗
Nursing & Feeding .... ✗
Safety & Babycare .... ✗
Clothing, Shoes & Accessories .... ✓
Books, Toys & Entertainment .... ✓

$$$ .... Prices
❸ .... Product availability
❸ .... Staff knowledge
❹ .... Customer service
❹ .... Decor

BALTIMORE—9000 FRANKLIN SQUARE DR (AT HOSPITAL DR); 443.777.7498; M-F 9:30-7:30 SA-SU 12-3:30

Gymboree

"...beautiful clothing and great quality... colorful and stylish baby and kids wear... lots of fun birthday gift ideas... easy exchange and return policy... items usually go on sale pretty quickly... save money with Gymbucks... many stores have a play area which makes shopping with my kids fun (let alone feasible)..."

Furniture, Bedding & Decor .... ✗
Gear & Equipment .... ✗

$$$ .... Prices
❹ .... Product availability

Nursing & Feeding ✗
Safety & Babycare ✗
Clothing, Shoes & Accessories ✓
Books, Toys & Entertainment ✓

❹ Staff knowledge
❹ Customer service
❹ Decor

WWW.GYMBOREE.COM

BALTIMORE—8200 PERRY HALL BLVD (AT HONEYGO BLVD); 410.931.4973; M-SA 10-9:30, SU 11-6; PARKING LOT

H & M ★★★½☆

"...wonderful prices for trendy baby and toddler clothes... it's the 'Euro' Target... buy for yourself and for your kids... a fun shopping experience as long as your child doesn't mind the bright lights and loud music... decent return policy... incredible sale prices... store can get messy at peak hours... busy and hectic, but their inventory is fun and worth the visit..."

Furniture, Bedding & Decor ✗
Gear & Equipment ✗
Nursing & Feeding ✗
Safety & Babycare ✗
Clothing, Shoes & Accessories ✓
Books, Toys & Entertainment ✓

$$ Prices
❸ Product availability
❸ Staff knowledge
❸ Customer service
❸ Decor

WWW.HM.COM

BALTIMORE—8200 PERRY HALL BLVD (AT HONEYGO BLVD); 410.931.9373; M-SA 10-9, SU 11-6

Hats to Hose ★★★☆☆

"...casual and formal wear for girls... helpful staff... pretty good selection, and reasonable prices..."

Furniture, Bedding & Decor ✗
Gear & Equipment ✗
Nursing & Feeding ✗
Safety & Babycare ✗
Clothing, Shoes & Accessories ✓
Books, Toys & Entertainment ✗

$$$$$ Prices
❸ Product availability
❹ Staff knowledge
❹ Customer service
❷ Decor

BALTIMORE—7002 REISTERSTOWN RD (AT FALLSTAFF RD); 410.484.7467; M-W 10-6, TH 10-8, F 10-3, SU 11-5; PARKING LOT

Hecht's ★★★☆☆

"...the baby department at Hecht's has a nice selection of moderately priced items... especially good selection for girl's clothes... the prices are right, but the service can be spotty... large and impersonal, messy racks, lack of service and style... pretty much your basic department store... good for baby gifts like picture frames and scrap books..."

Furniture, Bedding & Decor ✗
Gear & Equipment ✗
Nursing & Feeding ✗
Safety & Babycare ✗
Clothing, Shoes & Accessories ✓
Books, Toys & Entertainment ✓

$$$ Prices
❸ Product availability
❸ Staff knowledge
❸ Customer service
❸ Decor

WWW.HECHTS.COM

BALTIMORE—6901 SECURITY BLVD (AT SECURITY SQUARE MALL); 410.944.8040; CHECK SCHEDULE ONLINE; MALL PARKING

IKEA

"...the coolest-looking and best-priced bedding, bibs and eating utensils in town... fun, practical style and the prices are definitely right... one of the few stores around that lets kids climb and crawl on furniture... the kids' area has a slide, tunnels, tents... is it an indoor playground or a store?.. unending decorating ideas for families on a budget (lamps, rugs, beds, bedding)... it's all about organization—cubbies, drawers, shelves, seats that double as a trunk and step stool...

arts and crafts galore... free childcare while you shop... cheap eats if you get hungry... ”

Furniture, Bedding & Decor	✓	$$	Prices
Gear & Equipment	✗	❹	Product availability
Nursing & Feeding	✓	❹	Staff knowledge
Safety & Babycare	✓	❹	Customer service
Clothing, Shoes & Accessories	✗	❹	Decor
Books, Toys & Entertainment	✓		

WWW.IKEA.COM

BALTIMORE—8352 HONEYGO BLVD (AT WHITE MARSH MALL); 410.931.5400; M-F 10-9, SA 9-9, SU 10-8

JCPenney

“...always a good place to find clothes and other baby basics... the registry process was seamless... staff is generally friendly but the lines always seem long and slow... they don't have the greatest selection of toddler clothes, but their baby section is great... we had some damaged furniture delivered but customer service was easy and accommodating... a pretty limited selection of gear, but what they have is priced right... ”

Furniture, Bedding & Decor	✓	$$	Prices
Gear & Equipment	✓	❸	Product availability
Nursing & Feeding	✓	❸	Staff knowledge
Safety & Babycare	✓	❸	Customer service
Clothing, Shoes & Accessories	✓	❸	Decor
Books, Toys & Entertainment	✓		

WWW.JCPENNEY.COM

BALTIMORE—7777 EASTPOINT MALL (AT EASTPOINT MALL); 410.288.5800; M-F 9:30-9:30, SA 9-9:30, SU 11-6; PARKING LOT

KB Toys

“...hectic and always buzzing... wall-to-wall plastic and blinking lights... more Fisher-Price, Elmo and Sponge Bob than the eye can handle... a toy super store with discounted prices... they always have some kind of special sale going on... if you're looking for the latest and greatest popular toy, then look no further—not the place for unique or unusual toys... perfect for bulk toy shopping—especially around the holidays... ”

Furniture, Bedding & Decor	✗	$$	Prices
Gear & Equipment	✗	❸	Product availability
Nursing & Feeding	✗	❸	Staff knowledge
Safety & Babycare	✗	❸	Customer service
Clothing, Shoes & Accessories	✗	❸	Decor
Books, Toys & Entertainment	✓		

WWW.KBTOYS.COM

BALTIMORE—6901 SECURITY BLVD (AT SECURITY SQUARE MALL); 410.298.9692; M-SA 10-9:30, SU 12-6; MALL PARKING

BALTIMORE—NORTH POINT RD & EASTERN AVE (AT EASTPOINT MALL); 410.285.2565; M-SA 10-9, SU 12-6; MALL PARKING

Kid's Foot Locker

“...Nike, Reebok and Adidas for your little ones... hip, trendy and quite pricey... perfect for the sports addict dad who wants his kid sporting the latest NFL duds... shoes cost close to what the adult variety costs... generally good quality... they carry infant and toddler sizes... ”

Furniture, Bedding & Decor	✗	$$$	Prices
Gear & Equipment	✗	❸	Product availability
Nursing & Feeding	✗	❸	Staff knowledge
Safety & Babycare	✗	❸	Customer service
Clothing, Shoes & Accessories	✓	❸	Decor
Books, Toys & Entertainment	✗		

WWW.KIDSFOOTLOCKER.COM

BALTIMORE—2301 LIBERTY HEIGHTS AVE (AT N MONROE ST); 410.728.1928; M-SA 10-9, SU 12-5

BALTIMORE—7756 EASTPOINT MALL (AT NORTH POINT BLVD); 410.285.1290; M-SA 10-9, SU 12-6

Little Lamb Consignments

"...I love consignment shops... this store has super deals on books and toys, but the clothing selection is kinda lacking... not a lot of room so leave the stroller at home or in the car..."

Furniture, Bedding & Decor	✗	$$	Prices
Gear & Equipment	✗	4	Product availability
Nursing & Feeding	✗	4	Staff knowledge
Safety & Babycare	✗	3	Customer service
Clothing, Shoes & Accessories	✓	3	Decor
Books, Toys & Entertainment	✓		

BALTIMORE—5002 LAWNDALE AVE (AT WINDHURST AVE); 410.433.9086; T-W 10-4, TH 10-6, F 10-4, SA 10-6

Normal's Books & Records

"...normals is like a treasure chest for book lovers... fun area to walk and browse in... small children's book section, but it's worth a visit... you are sure to find a classic..."

Furniture, Bedding & Decor	✗	$	Prices
Gear & Equipment	✗	5	Product availability
Nursing & Feeding	✗	5	Staff knowledge
Safety & Babycare	✗	5	Customer service
Clothing, Shoes & Accessories	✗	4	Decor
Books, Toys & Entertainment	✓		

WWW.NORMALS.COM

BALTIMORE—425 E 31ST ST (AT GREENMOUNT ST); 410.243.6888; DAILY 11-6, SA 10-6; PARKING LOT

Old Navy

"...hip and 'in' clothes for infants and tots... plenty of steals on clearance items... T-shirts and pants for $10 or less... busy, busy, busy—long lines, especially on weekends... nothing fancy and you won't mind when your kids get down and dirty in these clothes... easy to wash, decent quality... you can shop for your baby, your toddler, your teen and yourself all at the same time... clothes are especially affordable when you hit their sales (post-holiday sales are amazing!)..."

Furniture, Bedding & Decor	✗	$$	Prices
Gear & Equipment	✗	4	Product availability
Nursing & Feeding	✗	3	Staff knowledge
Safety & Babycare	✗	3	Customer service
Clothing, Shoes & Accessories	✗	3	Decor
Books, Toys & Entertainment	✗		

WWW.OLDNAVY.COM

BALTIMORE—6901 SECURITY SQ BLVD (AT SECURITY SQ MALL); 443.436.5808; M-SA 10-9:30, SU 12-6

Payless Shoe Source

"...a good place for deals on children's shoes... staff is helpful with sizing... the selection and prices for kids' shoes can't be beat, but the quality isn't always spectacular... good leather shoes for cheap... great variety of all sizes and widths... I get my son's shoes here and don't feel like I'm wasting my money since he'll outgrow them in 3 months anyway..."

Furniture, Bedding & Decor	✗	$$	Prices
Gear & Equipment	✗	3	Product availability

Nursing & Feeding ✗
Safety & Babycare ✗
Clothing, Shoes & Accessories ✓
Books, Toys & Entertainment ✗

❸ Staff knowledge
❸ Customer service
❸ Decor

WWW.PAYLESS.COM

BALTIMORE—2112 E MONUMENT ST (AT N DUNCAN ST); 410.732.3787

BALTIMORE—311 W LEXINGTON ST (AT N HOWARD ST); 410.752.6061

BALTIMORE—ERDMAN SHOPPING AVE (AT N LUZERNE AVE); 410.276.1654

BALTIMORE—GALLERY AT HARBORPLACE (AT E MONUMENT ST); 410.962.0433; M-SA 10-9, SU 11-7

BALTIMORE—WESTSIDE SHOPPING CTR (AT RAMSAY ST); 410.362.5164; M-SA 10-8, SU 12-5

Pied Piper

"...the stuff that makes everyone say 'oooooooh' at a baby shower... beautiful infant layettes through boys and girls semi-casual wear... this store can't be beat for special clothes for your little one (or older child)... great selection of higher end everyday clothes... be sure to hit their big winter clearance—just get there early... beautiful gifts... bring your wallet loaded, but it's worth it..."

Furniture, Bedding & Decor ✗
Gear & Equipment ✗
Nursing & Feeding ✗
Safety & Babycare ✗
Clothing, Shoes & Accessories ✓
Books, Toys & Entertainment ✓

$$$$$ Prices
❹ Product availability
❹ Staff knowledge
❹ Customer service
❹ Decor

WWW.PIEDPIPERCHILDRENSWEAR.COM

BALTIMORE—32 VILLAGE SQ (AT CROSS KEYS RD); 410.435.2676; M-W F-SA 10-6; TH 10-8, SU 12-4; FREE PARKING

Rainbow Kids

"...fun clothing styles for infants and tots at low prices... the quality isn't the same as the more expensive brands, but the sleepers and play outfits always hold up well... great place for basics... cute trendy shoe selection for your little walker... we love the prices... up-to-date selection..."

Furniture, Bedding & Decor ✗
Gear & Equipment ✓
Nursing & Feeding ✗
Safety & Babycare ✗
Clothing, Shoes & Accessories ✓
Books, Toys & Entertainment ✓

$$ Prices
❸ Product availability
❸ Staff knowledge
❸ Customer service
❸ Decor

WWW.RAINBOWSHOPS.COM

BALTIMORE—1520 HAVENWOOD RD (AT LOCH RAVEN BLVD); 410.235.0681; DAILY 9-7

BALTIMORE—3901B ERDMAN AVE (AT SINCLAIR LN); 410.522.0490; M-W 10-8, TH-SA 10-9, SU 12-5

BALTIMORE—5628 THE ALAMEDA (AT WOODBOURNE AVE); 410.435.9240; M-SA 11-8 SU 11-5; PARKING LOT

BALTIMORE—6901 SECURITY BLVD (AT SECURITY SQUARE MALL); 410.277.9857; M-SA 10-9:30, SU 12-6; PARKING LOT

Raw Sugar

"...this store is all about fabulous kid stuff from hip maternity wear to Bratt Decor train tables... Milkshake CDs for the musical child... stretch mark lotion and a Fluerville diaper bag for me... perfect for unique gifts... unlike some ultrachic boutiques, the staff here are very friendly and helpful... a kids play gives me the couple of extra minutes I need... adorable kid's clothing, but limited sizes..."

Furniture, Bedding & Decor ✓
Gear & Equipment ✓

$$$$ Prices
❹ Product availability

Nursing & Feeding	✗	❹	Staff knowledge
Safety & Babycare	✗	❹	Customer service
Clothing, Shoes & Accessories	✓	❹	Decor
Books, Toys & Entertainment	✓		

WWW.RAWSUGARONLINE.COM

BALTIMORE—524 BELVEDERE AVE (AT YORK RD); 410.464.1240; M-SA 10-6, SU 11-5; STREET PARKING

Red Canoe ★★★★★

"...a place my toddler and I both love to hang out and shop... a lovely children's book selection—small, but well done... unbelievable muffins... fun story time tops off my favorite place to meet up with other moms..."

Furniture, Bedding & Decor	✗	$$	Prices
Gear & Equipment	✗	❹	Product availability
Nursing & Feeding	✗	❺	Staff knowledge
Safety & Babycare	✗	❺	Customer service
Clothing, Shoes & Accessories	✗	❹	Decor
Books, Toys & Entertainment	✓		

WWW.REDCANOE.BZ

BALTIMORE—4337 HARFORD RD (AT COLD SPRING LN); 410.444.4440; M-T 7:30-2, W-SA 7:30-5, SU 10-3; FREE PARKING

Sears ★★★☆☆

"...a decent selection of clothes and basic baby equipment... check out the Kids Club program—it's a great way to save money... you go to Sears to save money, not to be pampered... the quality of their merchandise is better than Wal-Mart, but don't expect anything too special or different... not much in terms of gear, but tons of well-priced baby and toddler clothing..."

Furniture, Bedding & Decor	✓	$$	Prices
Gear & Equipment	✓	❸	Product availability
Nursing & Feeding	✓	❸	Staff knowledge
Safety & Babycare	✓	❸	Customer service
Clothing, Shoes & Accessories	✓	❸	Decor
Books, Toys & Entertainment	✓		

WWW.SEARS.COM

BALTIMORE—6901 SECURITY BLVD (AT SECURITY SQ MALL OFF I-695); 410.281.2255; M-SA 10-9:30, SU 11-6; PARKING LOT

BALTIMORE—7885 EASTERN AVE (AT NORTH POINT BLVD); 410.288.7700; M-F 10-9, SA 8-6, SU 11-5; PARKING LOT

BALTIMORE—8200 PERRY HALL BLVD (AT HONEYGO BLVD); 410.931.5555; M-F 10-9, SA 10-6, SU 11-5; PARKING LOT

Shananigans ★★★☆☆

"...terrific selection of non-plastic toys... staff is super friendly and very knowledgeable... was able to find great gifts for a recent birthday party my son attended... free gift wrapping too... Tiny Love, Lamaze, Melissa and Doug, Manhattan Toys, Corolle and Goete Dolls, Calico Critters and tons more... on the pricey side, but you can definitely find something wonderful in your price range..."

Furniture, Bedding & Decor	✗	$$$	Prices
Gear & Equipment	✗	❹	Product availability
Nursing & Feeding	✗	❹	Staff knowledge
Safety & Babycare	✗	❹	Customer service
Clothing, Shoes & Accessories	✗	❸	Decor
Books, Toys & Entertainment	✓		

BALTIMORE—5004 B LAWNDALE AVE (AT WYNDHURST AVE); 410.532.8384; M-SA 10-5; STREET PARKING

Su Casa

Furniture, Bedding & Decor	✓	✗	Gear & Equipment
Nursing & Feeding	✗	✗	Safety & Babycare
Clothing, Shoes & Accessories	✗	✗	Books, Toys & Entertainment

WWW.ESUCASA.COM

BALTIMORE—901 S BOND ST (AT THAMES ST); 410.522.7010; M-TH 10-9, F-SA 10-11, SU 10-8

Talbots Kids

"...a nice alternative to the typical department store experience... expensive, but fantastic quality... great for holiday and special occasion outfits including christening outfits... well-priced, conservative children's clothing... cute selections for infants, toddlers and kids... sales are fantastic—up to half off at least a couple times a year... the best part is, you can also shop for yourself while shopping for baby..."

Furniture, Bedding & Decor	✗	$$$$	Prices
Gear & Equipment	✗	4	Product availability
Nursing & Feeding	✗	4	Staff knowledge
Safety & Babycare	✗	4	Customer service
Clothing, Shoes & Accessories	✓	4	Decor
Books, Toys & Entertainment	✗		

WWW.TALBOTS.COM

BALTIMORE—50 VILLAGE SQUARE (AT FALLS RD); 410.323.5166; M-F 10-7, SA 10-6, SU 12-5; PARKING LOT

Target

"...our favorite place to shop for kids' stuff—good selection and very affordable... guilt-free shopping—kids grow so fast so I don't want to pay high department-store prices... everything from diapers and sippy cups to car seats and strollers... easy return policy... generally helpful staff, but you don't go for the service—you go for the prices... decent registry that won't freak your friends out with outrageous prices... easy, convenient shopping for well-priced items... all the big-box brands available—Graco, Evenflo, Eddie Bauer, etc...."

Furniture, Bedding & Decor	✓	$$	Prices
Gear & Equipment	✓	4	Product availability
Nursing & Feeding	✓	3	Staff knowledge
Safety & Babycare	✓	3	Customer service
Clothing, Shoes & Accessories	✓	3	Decor
Books, Toys & Entertainment	✓		

WWW.TARGET.COM

BALTIMORE—5230 CAMPBELL BLVD (AT I 95); 410.933.9632; M-SA 8-10, SU 8-9; PARKING LOT

The Circle Shop

"...an excellent shop with a wide variety of used baby clothing and equipment... I remember my mom shopping here when I was little... lots of clothes and lots of everything secondhand... the women who run it are the best..."

Furniture, Bedding & Decor	✗	$$	Prices
Gear & Equipment	✗	4	Product availability
Nursing & Feeding	✗	4	Staff knowledge
Safety & Babycare	✗	4	Customer service
Clothing, Shoes & Accessories	✓	4	Decor
Books, Toys & Entertainment	✗		

BALTIMORE—6124 BELAIR RD (AT GLENNMORE); 410.254.6066; M W-SA 10-4; PARKING LOT

The Corduroy Button

"...the coolest baby and kid's clothing... I have no idea where they find such fabulous clothes... nice sales staff... an earthy feel to their stuff... my favorite shop for gifts..."

Furniture, Bedding & Decor	✗	$$$$	Prices
Gear & Equipment	✗	❹	Product availability
Nursing & Feeding	✗	❹	Staff knowledge
Safety & Babycare	✗	❹	Customer service
Clothing, Shoes & Accessories	✓	❹	Decor
Books, Toys & Entertainment	✗		

BALTIMORE—1628 THAMES ST (AT BROADWAY); 410.276.5437; M-TH 10-8, SA-SU 10-9 ; PARKING LOT

Toys R Us

"...not just toys, but also tons of gear and supplies including diapers and formula... a hectic shopping experience but the prices make it all worthwhile... I've experienced good and bad service at the same store on the same day... the stores are huge and can be overwhelming... most big brand-names available... leave the kids at home unless you want to end up with a cart full of toys..."

Furniture, Bedding & Decor	✓	$$$	Prices
Gear & Equipment	✓	❹	Product availability
Nursing & Feeding	✓	❸	Staff knowledge
Safety & Babycare	✓	❸	Customer service
Clothing, Shoes & Accessories	✓	❸	Decor
Books, Toys & Entertainment	✓		

WWW.TOYSRUS.COM

BALTIMORE—1238 PUTTY HILL AVE (AT TOWNSON PLACE); 410.823.8877; M-SA 10-9, SU 10-6; PARKING LOT

BALTIMORE—8804 PULASKI HWY (AT ROSEVILLE BLVD); 410.682.5166; M-SA 10-9, SU 10-6; PARKING LOT

Value City

"...if you are looking for bargain merchandise for the whole family, you'll find it here... you can always find something and lots of inexpensive baby and toddler clothes... very low prices with many sizes... chaotic atmosphere and hard to find staff, once you do they are very helpful... lines can be long..."

Furniture, Bedding & Decor	✓	$$	Prices
Gear & Equipment	✓	❸	Product availability
Nursing & Feeding	✓	❸	Staff knowledge
Safety & Babycare	✓	❸	Customer service
Clothing, Shoes & Accessories	✓	❸	Decor
Books, Toys & Entertainment	✓		

WWW.VALUECITY.COM

BALTIMORE—7735 EASTPOINT MALL (AT N PT BLVD); 410.282.8295; M-SA 9:30-9, SU 11-6

Wyndhurst Seperates

"...fabulous maternity clothes... very trendy... pricey, but catch the sales and you're bound to find some great deals... good for gifts or a little treat for yourself or baby..."

Furniture, Bedding & Decor	✗	$$$$	Prices
Gear & Equipment	✗	❸	Product availability
Nursing & Feeding	✗	❹	Staff knowledge
Safety & Babycare	✗	❹	Customer service
Clothing, Shoes & Accessories	✓	❹	Decor
Books, Toys & Entertainment	✗		

BALTIMORE—5002 LAWNDALE AVE (AT WYNDHURST STATION); 410.377.8030; M-W 10-5, TH 10-8, F-SA 10-5, SU 12-4; PARKING LOT

North of Baltimore

April Cornell

"...beautiful, classic dresses and accessories for special occasions... I love the matching 'mommy and me' outfits... lots of fun knickknacks for sale... great selection of baby wear on their web site... rest assured your baby won't look like every other child in these adorable outfits... very frilly and girlie—beautiful..."

Furniture, Bedding & Decor	✗	$$$	Prices
Gear & Equipment	✗	❸	Product availability
Nursing & Feeding	✗	❹	Staff knowledge
Safety & Babycare	✗	❹	Customer service
Clothing, Shoes & Accessories	✓	❹	Decor
Books, Toys & Entertainment	✗		

TOWSON—825 DULANEY VALLEY RD (AT TOWSON TOWN CENTER); 410.823.0833; M-SA 10-9:30, SU 11-6

Baby Depot At Burlington Coat Factory

"...a large, 'super store' layout with a ton of baby gear... wide aisles, packed shelves, barely existent customer service and awesome prices... everything from bottles, car seats and strollers to gliders, cribs and clothes... I always find something worth getting... a little disorganized and hard to locate items you're looking for... the staff is not always knowledgeable about their merchandise... return policy is store credit only..."

Furniture, Bedding & Decor	✓	$$	Prices
Gear & Equipment	✓	❸	Product availability
Nursing & Feeding	✓	❸	Staff knowledge
Safety & Babycare	✓	❸	Customer service
Clothing, Shoes & Accessories	✓	❸	Decor
Books, Toys & Entertainment	✓		

WWW.BABYDEPOT.COM

HUNT VALLEY—118 SHAWAN RD (AT HUNT VALLEY MALL); 410.584.7407; M-SA 10-9:30, SU 11-6

BabyGap/GapKids

"...colorful baby and toddler clothing in clean, well-lit stores... great return policy... it's the Gap, so you know what you're getting—colorful, cute and well-made clothing... best place for baby hats... prices are reasonable especially since there's always a sale of some sort going on... sales, sales, sales—frequent and fantastic... everything I'm looking for in infant clothing—snap crotches, snaps up the front, all natural fabrics and great styling... fun seasonal selections—a great place to shop for gifts as well as for your own kids... although it can get busy, staff generally seem accommodating and helpful..."

Furniture, Bedding & Decor	✗	$$$	Prices
Gear & Equipment	✗	❹	Product availability
Nursing & Feeding	✗	❹	Staff knowledge
Safety & Babycare	✗	❹	Customer service
Clothing, Shoes & Accessories	✓	❹	Decor
Books, Toys & Entertainment	✗		

WWW.GAP.COM

TOWSON—825 DULANEY VALLEY RD (AT TOWNSON TOWN CTR); 410.494.0903; M-SA 10-9:30, SU 11-6; PARKING LOT

Baltimore Medical Center Corner Gift Shop

"...hospital gift store... adorable baby items... perfect for the last minute gift when you're running up to visit mom and the new baby... I found the cutest things to bring home to my daughter... it makes the hospital experience so much better... free gift wrapping..."

Furniture, Bedding & Decor	✗	$$$	Prices
Gear & Equipment	✗	❹	Product availability
Nursing & Feeding	✗	❹	Staff knowledge
Safety & Babycare	✗	❹	Customer service
Clothing, Shoes & Accessories	✗	❺	Decor
Books, Toys & Entertainment	✓		

WWW.GBMC.ORG

TOWSON—6701 N CHARLES ST (AT TOWNSEND BLVD); 443.849.2135; M-TH 7-8, F 7-7, SA 11:30-4, SU 12-4:30; PARKING LOT

Book Rack

"...will buy your used books at half the publisher's listed price... they give store credit which I easily spend... they have a terrific selection of children's books..."

Furniture, Bedding & Decor	✗	$	Prices
Gear & Equipment	✗	❸	Product availability
Nursing & Feeding	✗	❺	Staff knowledge
Safety & Babycare	✗	❺	Customer service
Clothing, Shoes & Accessories	✗	❺	Decor
Books, Toys & Entertainment	✓		

TIMONIUM—55 E PADONIA RD (AT YORK RD); 410.667.6897; M 10-8, T-SA 10-6, SU 12-4; PARKING LOT

Greetings & Readings

Furniture, Bedding & Decor	✗	✗	Gear & Equipment
Nursing & Feeding	✗	✗	Safety & Babycare
Clothing, Shoes & Accessories	✗	✗	Books, Toys & Entertainment

WWW.GREETINGSANDREADINGS.COM

TOWSON—118-AA SHAWAN ROA (BTWN YORK AND I-83); 410.771.3022; M-TH 10-9:30, F-SA 10-10:30, SU 11-8; PARKING LOT

Growing Up Shoppes

"...this is where to get the important outfits—christening, birthdays, parties, etc... so adorable... Lilly Pulitzer and Ralph Lauren designs... I love this place for specialty outfits and for gifts... cute and unique clothes with wonderful salespeople... pricey, but decent sales about twice a year..."

Furniture, Bedding & Decor	✗	$$$$	Prices
Gear & Equipment	✗	❹	Product availability
Nursing & Feeding	✗	❹	Staff knowledge
Safety & Babycare	✗	❹	Customer service
Clothing, Shoes & Accessories	✓	❹	Decor
Books, Toys & Entertainment	✗		

TOWSON—858 KENILWORTH DR (AT STONEWAIN CT); 410.339.7840; M-F 10-9, SA 10-8, SU 12-5

Gymboree

"...beautiful clothing and great quality... colorful and stylish baby and kids wear... lots of fun birthday gift ideas... easy exchange and return policy... items usually go on sale pretty quickly... save money with Gymbucks... many stores have a play area which makes shopping with my kids fun (let alone feasible)..."

Furniture, Bedding & Decor	✗	$$$	Prices
Gear & Equipment	✗	❹	Product availability

Nursing & Feeding	✗	❹	Staff knowledge
Safety & Babycare	✗	❹	Customer service
Clothing, Shoes & Accessories	✓	❹	Decor
Books, Toys & Entertainment	✓		

WWW.GYMBOREE.COM

TOWSON—825 DULANEY VALLEY RD (AT TOWSON TOWN CTR); 410.821.8958; M-SA 10-9:30, SU 11-6; PARKING LOT

Hecht's

"...the baby department at Hecht's has a nice selection of moderately priced items... especially good selection for girl's clothes... the prices are right, but the service can be spotty... large and impersonal, messy racks, lack of service and style... pretty much your basic department store... good for baby gifts like picture frames and scrap books..."

Furniture, Bedding & Decor	✗	$$$	Prices
Gear & Equipment	✗	❸	Product availability
Nursing & Feeding	✗	❸	Staff knowledge
Safety & Babycare	✗	❸	Customer service
Clothing, Shoes & Accessories	✓	❸	Decor
Books, Toys & Entertainment	✓		

WWW.HECHTS.COM

BEL AIR—600 BELAIR RD (AT BEL AIRL); 410.879.9801; CHECK SCHEDULE ONLINE; FREE PARKING

TOWSON—813 DULANEY VALLEY RD (AT TOWSON TOWN CTR); 410.337.3600; CHECK SCHEDULE ONLINE

KB Toys

"...hectic and always buzzing... wall-to-wall plastic and blinking lights... more Fisher-Price, Elmo and Sponge Bob than the eye can handle... a toy super store with discounted prices... they always have some kind of special sale going on... if you're looking for the latest and greatest popular toy, then look no further—not the place for unique or unusual toys... perfect for bulk toy shopping—especially around the holidays..."

Furniture, Bedding & Decor	✗	$$	Prices
Gear & Equipment	✗	❸	Product availability
Nursing & Feeding	✗	❸	Staff knowledge
Safety & Babycare	✗	❸	Customer service
Clothing, Shoes & Accessories	✗	❸	Decor
Books, Toys & Entertainment	✓		

WWW.KBTOYS.COM

BEL AIR—698 BELAIR RD (AT S TOLLGATE RD); 410.836.5637; DAILY 10-9; MALL PARKING

Kid's Foot Locker

"...Nike, Reebok and Adidas for your little ones... hip, trendy and quite pricey... perfect for the sports addict dad who wants his kid sporting the latest NFL duds... shoes cost close to what the adult variety costs... generally good quality... they carry infant and toddler sizes..."

Furniture, Bedding & Decor	✗	$$$	Prices
Gear & Equipment	✗	❸	Product availability
Nursing & Feeding	✗	❸	Staff knowledge
Safety & Babycare	✗	❸	Customer service
Clothing, Shoes & Accessories	✓	❸	Decor
Books, Toys & Entertainment	✗		

WWW.KIDSFOOTLOCKER.COM

TOWSON—825 DULANEY VALLEY RD (AT FAIRMONT AVE); 410.828.5320; M-SA 10-9:30, SU 11-6

Kohl's

"...nice one-stop shopping for the whole family—everything from clothing to baby gear... great sales on clothing and a good selection of higher-end brands... stylish, inexpensive clothes for babies through 24 months... very easy shopping experience... dirt-cheap sales and clearance prices... nothing super fancy, but just right for those everyday romper outfits... Graco, Eddie Bauer and other well-known brands..."

Furniture, Bedding & Decor	✓	$$	Prices
Gear & Equipment	✓	❹	Product availability
Nursing & Feeding	✓	❸	Staff knowledge
Safety & Babycare	✓	❸	Customer service
Clothing, Shoes & Accessories	✓	❸	Decor
Books, Toys & Entertainment	✓		

WWW.KOHLS.COM

BEL AIR—5 BEL AIR S PKWY (AT EMMORTON RD); 410.569.6066; M-SA 8-10, SU 10-8

Lord & Lady Bug

"...unique and adorable clothes and accessories... expensive, but high-quality and nice gift wrapping... terrific sales and great service... special occasion outfits... terrific quality to go along with the higher prices..."

Furniture, Bedding & Decor	✗	$$$$	Prices
Gear & Equipment	✗	❸	Product availability
Nursing & Feeding	✗	❹	Staff knowledge
Safety & Babycare	✗	❸	Customer service
Clothing, Shoes & Accessories	✓	❹	Decor
Books, Toys & Entertainment	✗		

LUTHERVILLE—10751 FALLS RD (AT GREENSPRING VALLEY RD); 410.832.5437; M-F 10-6, SA 10-5

Marshalls

"...the ultimate hit or miss... you can generally find all the basics—pajamas, onesies, and booties for a fraction of the regular price... I love to browse the toy aisle for inexpensive shower and birthday gifts... I only go when I am feeling patient and persistent... the aisles are crammed with goods..."

Furniture, Bedding & Decor	✗	$$	Prices
Gear & Equipment	✗	❸	Product availability
Nursing & Feeding	✗	❷	Staff knowledge
Safety & Babycare	✗	❷	Customer service
Clothing, Shoes & Accessories	✓	❸	Decor
Books, Toys & Entertainment	✓		

WWW.MARSHALLS.COM

TOWSON—1238 PUTTY HILL AVE (AT TOWSON PLACE); 410.825.0350; M-SA 9:30-9:30 SU 11-6 ; PARKING LOT

Nordstrom

"...quality service and quality clothes... awesome kids shoe department—almost as good as the one for adults... free balloons in the children's shoe area as well as drawing tables... in addition to their own brand, they carry a very nice selection of other high-end baby clothing including Ralph Lauren, Robeez, etc... adorable baby clothes—they make great shower gifts... such a wonderful shopping experience—their lounge is perfect for breastfeeding and for changing diapers... well-rounded selection of baby basics as well as fancy clothes for special events..."

Furniture, Bedding & Decor	✓	$$$$	Prices
Gear & Equipment	✓	❹	Product availability
Nursing & Feeding	✗	❹	Staff knowledge
Safety & Babycare	✗	❹	Customer service
Clothing, Shoes & Accessories	✓	❹	Decor

Books, Toys & Entertainment ....✓

WWW.NORDSTROM.COM

TOWSON—700 FAIRMOUNT AVE (AT TOWSON TOWN CTR); 410.296.2111; M-SA 10-9:30, SU 11-6

Old Navy

"...hip and 'in' clothes for infants and tots... plenty of steals on clearance items... T-shirts and pants for $10 or less... busy, busy, busy—long lines, especially on weekends... nothing fancy and you won't mind when your kids get down and dirty in these clothes... easy to wash, decent quality... you can shop for your baby, your toddler, your teen and yourself all at the same time... clothes are especially affordable when you hit their sales (post-holiday sales are amazing!)..."

Furniture, Bedding & Decor .... ✗ | $$ .... Prices
Gear & Equipment .... ✗ | ❹ .... Product availability
Nursing & Feeding .... ✗ | ❸ .... Staff knowledge
Safety & Babycare .... ✗ | ❸ .... Customer service
Clothing, Shoes & Accessories .... ✓ | ❸ .... Decor
Books, Toys & Entertainment .... ✗

WWW.OLDNAVY.COM

BEL AIR—678 BEL AIR RD (AT HARFORD MALL); 410.638.6780; M-SA 10-9:30, SU 11-5; PARKING LOT

LUTHERVILLE—170 W RIDGELY RD (AT RTE 45); 410.666.0538; M-SA 9-9, SU 10-6

Robyn's Nest Clothing

Furniture, Bedding & Decor .... ✗ | ✗ .... Gear & Equipment
Nursing & Feeding .... ✗ | ✗ .... Safety & Babycare
Clothing, Shoes & Accessories .... ✗ | ✗ .... Books, Toys & Entertainment

COCKEYSVILLE—10872 YORK RD (AT SHERWOOD RD); 410.628.0300

Ross Dress For Less

"...if you're in the mood for bargain hunting and are okay with potentially coming up empty-handed, then Ross is for you... don't expect to get educated about baby products here... go early on a week day and you'll find an organized store and staff that is helpful and available—forget weekends... their selection is pretty inconsistent, but I have found some incredible bargains... a great place to stock up on birthday presents or stocking stuffers..."

Furniture, Bedding & Decor .... ✗ | $$ .... Prices
Gear & Equipment .... ✗ | ❸ .... Product availability
Nursing & Feeding .... ✗ | ❸ .... Staff knowledge
Safety & Babycare .... ✗ | ❸ .... Customer service
Clothing, Shoes & Accessories .... ✓ | ❸ .... Decor
Books, Toys & Entertainment .... ✓

WWW.ROSSSTORES.COM

PARKVILLE—8888 WALTHAM WOODS RD (AT PERRING PKWY); 410.661.7390; M-SA 9:30-9:30, SU 11-7; PARKING LOT

Sears

"...a decent selection of clothes and basic baby equipment... check out the Kids Club program—it's a great way to save money... you go to Sears to save money, not to be pampered... the quality of their merchandise is better than Wal-Mart, but don't expect anything too special or different... not much in terms of gear, but tons of well-priced baby and toddler clothing..."

Furniture, Bedding & Decor .... ✓ | $$ .... Prices
Gear & Equipment .... ✓ | ❸ .... Product availability
Nursing & Feeding .... ✓ | ❸ .... Staff knowledge
Safety & Babycare .... ✓ | ❸ .... Customer service

Clothing, Shoes & Accessories ...... ✓
Books, Toys & Entertainment .... ✓

❸ .... Decor

WWW.SEARS.COM

BEL AIR—658 BALTIMORE PIKE (AT HARFORD MALL); 410.588.5000; M-F 9:30-9:30, SA 9-10, SU 10-6; PARKING LOT

COCKEYSVILLE—126 SHAWAN RD (AT YORK RD); 410.771.8355; M-F 9:30-9:30, SA 8-9:30, SU 10-6; PARKING LOT

Small Wonders ★★★☆☆

"...great toy store... anything and everything from babies to preteens... wind up, dress up, Thomas the Train, Playmobile, jewelry making kits, arts and crafts, fire engines, baby toys... perfect place to shop for a birthday gift... look for coupons in their catalog..."

Furniture, Bedding & Decor .... ✗
Gear & Equipment .... ✗
Nursing & Feeding .... ✗
Safety & Babycare .... ✗
Clothing, Shoes & Accessories .... ✗
Books, Toys & Entertainment .... ✓

$$$ .... Prices
❸ .... Product availability
❸ .... Staff knowledge
❸ .... Customer service
❸ .... Decor

PHOENIX—3417 SWEET AIR RD (AT HWY 146); 410.628.1600; M-F 10-6, SA 10-5, SU 11-3

Talbots Kids ★★★½☆

"...a nice alternative to the typical department store experience... expensive, but fantastic quality... great for holiday and special occasion outfits including christening outfits... well-priced, conservative children's clothing... cute selections for infants, toddlers and kids... sales are fantastic—up to half off at least a couple times a year... the best part is, you can also shop for yourself while shopping for baby..."

Furniture, Bedding & Decor .... ✗
Gear & Equipment .... ✗
Nursing & Feeding .... ✗
Safety & Babycare .... ✗
Clothing, Shoes & Accessories ...... ✓
Books, Toys & Entertainment .... ✗

$$$$ .... Prices
❹ .... Product availability
❹ .... Staff knowledge
❹ .... Customer service
❹ .... Decor

WWW.TALBOTS.COM

COCKEYSVILLE—10265 YORK RD (AT SCOTT ADAM RD); 410.666.0596; M-SA 10-8, SU 12-5

TOWSON—825 DULANEY VALLEY RD (AT TOWSON TWON CTR); 410.823.1640; M-SA 10-9:30 SU 11-6; PARKING LOT

Target ★★★★☆

"...our favorite place to shop for kids' stuff—good selection and very affordable... guilt-free shopping—kids grow so fast so I don't want to pay high department-store prices... everything from diapers and sippy cups to car seats and strollers... easy return policy... generally helpful staff, but you don't go for the service—you go for the prices... decent registry that won't freak your friends out with outrageous prices... easy, convenient shopping for well-priced items... all the big-box brands available—Graco, Evenflo, Eddie Bauer, etc...."

Furniture, Bedding & Decor .... ✓
Gear & Equipment .... ✓
Nursing & Feeding .... ✓
Safety & Babycare .... ✓
Clothing, Shoes & Accessories ...... ✓
Books, Toys & Entertainment .... ✓

$$ .... Prices
❹ .... Product availability
❸ .... Staff knowledge
❸ .... Customer service
❸ .... Decor

WWW.TARGET.COM

BEL AIR—580 MARKETPLACE DR (AT HWY 24); 410.638.7532; M-SA 8-10, SU 8-9

TOWSON—1238 PUTTY HILL AVE (AT TOWSON PL); 410.823.4423; M-SA 8-10, SU 8-9; PARKING LOT

Towson Bootery

"...the shoe store for the discriminating tot shoe shopper... great selection... patient and helpful staff..."

Furniture, Bedding & Decor	✗	$$$	Prices
Gear & Equipment	✗	4	Product availability
Nursing & Feeding	✗	4	Staff knowledge
Safety & Babycare	✗	4	Customer service
Clothing, Shoes & Accessories	✓	4	Decor
Books, Toys & Entertainment	✗		

TOWSON—810 KENILWORTH DR (AT WEST RD); 410.296.0640; M-SA 10-9, SU 12-5; PARKING LOT

Toys R Us

"...not just toys, but also tons of gear and supplies including diapers and formula... a hectic shopping experience but the prices make it all worthwhile... I've experienced good and bad service at the same store on the same day... the stores are huge and can be overwhelming... most big brand-names available... leave the kids at home unless you want to end up with a cart full of toys..."

Furniture, Bedding & Decor	✓	$$$	Prices
Gear & Equipment	✓	4	Product availability
Nursing & Feeding	✓	3	Staff knowledge
Safety & Babycare	✓	3	Customer service
Clothing, Shoes & Accessories	✓	3	Decor
Books, Toys & Entertainment	✓		

WWW.TOYSRUS.COM

BEL AIR—660 MARKETPLACE DR (AT ROUTE 24); 410.838.0010; M-SA 10-9 SU 10-6 ; PARKING LOT

Tried But True

"...if you happen to be in the shop at the right time you just might find a fabulous gem at a super price... hit or miss... they carry maternity, baby and children's clothing... toys and baby equipment too... this consignment store carries the top brands at really discounted prices..."

Furniture, Bedding & Decor	✗	$	Prices
Gear & Equipment	✓	4	Product availability
Nursing & Feeding	✗	5	Staff knowledge
Safety & Babycare	✗	5	Customer service
Clothing, Shoes & Accessories	✓	4	Decor
Books, Toys & Entertainment	✓		

COCKEYSVILLE—10744 YORK RD (AT ROBERTS RD); 410.666.9265; M W F-SA 10-4, T TH 10-5, SU 12-5; PARKING LOT

West of Baltimore

"lila picks"

★Elephant's Trunk

Babies R Us

"...everything baby under one roof... they have a wide selection and carry most 'mainstream' items such as Graco, Fisher-Price, Avent and Britax... great customer service—given how big the stores are, I was pleasantly surprised at how attentive the staff was... easy return policy... super busy on weekends so try to visit on a weekday for the best service... keep an eye out for great coupons, deals and frequent sales... easy and comprehensive registry... shopping here is so easy—you've got to check it out..."

Furniture, Bedding & Decor	✓	$$$	Prices
Gear & Equipment	✓	❹	Product availability
Nursing & Feeding	✓	❹	Staff knowledge
Safety & Babycare	✓	❹	Customer service
Clothing, Shoes & Accessories	✓	❹	Decor
Books, Toys & Entertainment	✓		

WWW.BABIESRUS.COM

CATONSVILLE—6501 BALTIMORE PIKE (AT N ROLLING RD); 410.744.0820; M-SA 9:30-9:30, SU 11-7; PARKING LOT

Baby Basics

"...new, local baby supply store... knowledgeable staff and great product selection... this place has everything and if they don't, just ask and they will find it for you... the owner is available and happy to give his opinion... check it out..."

Furniture, Bedding & Decor	✓	$$$	Prices
Gear & Equipment	✓	❹	Product availability
Nursing & Feeding	✓	❹	Staff knowledge
Safety & Babycare	✓	❹	Customer service
Clothing, Shoes & Accessories	✓	❸	Decor
Books, Toys & Entertainment	✓		

PIKESVILLE—1400 REISTERSTOWN RD (AT WALKER AVE); 410.486.4100; M-T TH 10-6, W 10-8, SU 10-4

Big Lots

"...I was amazed to find such discounts on brand items... big items at small prices... great, functional low-priced furniture for kids, now where can you find that?... better for kids than babies... a little dirty... same products as the department stores... I did most of my Christmas shopping here..."

Furniture, Bedding & Decor	✓	$$	Prices
Gear & Equipment	✗	❸	Product availability
Nursing & Feeding	✗	❸	Staff knowledge
Safety & Babycare	✗	❸	Customer service
Clothing, Shoes & Accessories	✗	❸	Decor

Books, Toys & Entertainment .... ×

WWW.BIGLOTS.COM

REISTERSTOWN—11716 REISTERSTOWN RD (AT E CHERRY HILL RD); 410.526.9244; M-SA 9-9, SU 9-8

Children's Place, The

“...great bargains on cute clothing... shoes, socks, swimsuits, sunglasses and everything in between... lots of '3 for $20' type deals on sleepers, pants and mix-and-match separates... so much more affordable than the other 'big chains'... don't expect the most unique stuff here, but it wears and washes well... cheap clothing for cheap prices... you can leave the store with bags full of clothes without putting a huge dent in your wallet...”

Furniture, Bedding & Decor	×	$$	Prices
Gear & Equipment	×	❹	Product availability
Nursing & Feeding	×	❹	Staff knowledge
Safety & Babycare	×	❹	Customer service
Clothing, Shoes & Accessories	✓	❹	Decor
Books, Toys & Entertainment	✓		

WWW.CHILDRENSPLACE.COM

OWINGS MILLS—10300 MILL RUN CIR (AT OWINGS MILLS TOWN CTR); 410.363.0277; M-SA 10-9, SU 12-6; FREE PARKING

Elephant's Trunk

“...a cute consignment shop with gently-used toys, baby gear, and furniture... great for toys for Grandma's house!.. perfect for those on a budget... my favorite consignment shop in the Baltimore area... in gets quite crowded in there... lovely owner makes consigning here a pleasure...”

Furniture, Bedding & Decor	✓	$$	Prices
Gear & Equipment	✓	❹	Product availability
Nursing & Feeding	×	❹	Staff knowledge
Safety & Babycare	✓	❹	Customer service
Clothing, Shoes & Accessories	✓	❸	Decor
Books, Toys & Entertainment	✓		

REISTERSTOWN—317 MAIN ST (AT BOND AVE); 410.517.1200; W-F 11-5, SA 11-4, SU 12-4

Gymboree

“...beautiful clothing and great quality... colorful and stylish baby and kids wear... lots of fun birthday gift ideas... easy exchange and return policy... items usually go on sale pretty quickly... save money with Gymbucks... many stores have a play area which makes shopping with my kids fun (let alone feasible)...”

Furniture, Bedding & Decor	×	$$$	Prices
Gear & Equipment	×	❹	Product availability
Nursing & Feeding	×	❹	Staff knowledge
Safety & Babycare	×	❹	Customer service
Clothing, Shoes & Accessories	✓	❹	Decor
Books, Toys & Entertainment	✓		

WWW.GYMBOREE.COM

OWINGS MILLS—10300 MILL RUN CIR (AT OWINGS MALL TOWN CTR); 410.356.5578; M-SA 10-9:30, SU 11-6; MALL PARKING

H & M

“...wonderful prices for trendy baby and toddler clothes... it's the 'Euro' Target... buy for yourself and for your kids... a fun shopping experience as long as your child doesn't mind the bright lights and loud music... decent return policy... incredible sale prices... store can get messy at peak hours... busy and hectic, but their inventory is fun and worth the visit...”

Furniture, Bedding & Decor .... ✗
Gear & Equipment .... ✗
Nursing & Feeding .... ✗
Safety & Babycare .... ✗
Clothing, Shoes & Accessories ...... ✓
Books, Toys & Entertainment .... ✓

$$ .... Prices
❸ .... Product availability
❸ .... Staff knowledge
❸ .... Customer service
❸ .... Decor

WWW.HM.COM

OWINGS MILLS—10300 MILL RUN CIR (AT OWINGS MILLS TOWN CTR); 443.394.0291; M-SA 10-9, SU 11-6

Hecht's ★★★☆☆

"...the baby department at Hecht's has a nice selection of moderately priced items... especially good selection for girl's clothes... the prices are right, but the service can be spotty... large and impersonal, messy racks, lack of service and style... pretty much your basic department store... good for baby gifts like picture frames and scrap books..."

Furniture, Bedding & Decor .... ✗
Gear & Equipment .... ✗
Nursing & Feeding .... ✗
Safety & Babycare .... ✗
Clothing, Shoes & Accessories ...... ✓
Books, Toys & Entertainment .... ✓

$$$ .... Prices
❸ .... Product availability
❸ .... Staff knowledge
❸ .... Customer service
❸ .... Decor

WWW.HECHTS.COM

OWINGS MILLS—10300 MILL RUN CIR (AT OWINGS MILLS TOWN CTR); 410.363.7700; CHECK SCHEDULE ONLINE

JCPenney ★★★½☆

"...always a good place to find clothes and other baby basics... the registry process was seamless... staff is generally friendly but the lines always seem long and slow... they don't have the greatest selection of toddler clothes, but their baby section is great... we had some damaged furniture delivered but customer service was easy and accommodating... a pretty limited selection of gear, but what they have is priced right..."

Furniture, Bedding & Decor .... ✓
Gear & Equipment .... ✓
Nursing & Feeding .... ✓
Safety & Babycare .... ✓
Clothing, Shoes & Accessories ...... ✓
Books, Toys & Entertainment .... ✓

$$ .... Prices
❸ .... Product availability
❸ .... Staff knowledge
❸ .... Customer service
❸ .... Decor

WWW.JCPENNEY.COM

OWINGS MILLS—10400 MILL RUN CIR (AT OWINGS MILLS BLVD); 410.902.9400; M-SA 10-9:30, SU 11-7; PARKING LOT

Macy's ★★★½☆

"...Macy's has it all and I never leave empty-handed... if you time your visit right you can find some great deals... go during the week so you don't get overwhelmed with the weekend crowd... good for staples as well as beautiful party dresses for girls... lots of brand-names like Carter's, Guess, and Ralph Lauren... not much in terms of assistance... newspaper coupons and sales help keep the cost down... some stores are better organized and maintained than others... if you're going to shop at a department store for your baby, then Macy's is a safe bet..."

Furniture, Bedding & Decor .... ✓
Gear & Equipment .... ✗
Nursing & Feeding .... ✗
Safety & Babycare .... ✗
Clothing, Shoes & Accessories ...... ✓
Books, Toys & Entertainment .... ✓

$$$ .... Prices
❸ .... Product availability
❸ .... Staff knowledge
❸ .... Customer service
❸ .... Decor

WWW.MACYS.COM

OWINGS MILLS—10200 MILL RUN CIR (AT OWING MILLS TOWN CTR); 410.363.7400; M-TH 10-9:30, F-SA 10-10, SU 11-6

Ross Dress For Less

"...if you're in the mood for bargain hunting and are okay with potentially coming up empty-handed, then Ross is for you... don't expect to get educated about baby products here... go early on a week day and you'll find an organized store and staff that is helpful and available—forget weekends... their selection is pretty inconsistent, but I have found some incredible bargains... a great place to stock up on birthday presents or stocking stuffers..."

Furniture, Bedding & Decor	✗	$$	Prices
Gear & Equipment	✗	3	Product availability
Nursing & Feeding	✗	3	Staff knowledge
Safety & Babycare	✗	3	Customer service
Clothing, Shoes & Accessories	✓	3	Decor
Books, Toys & Entertainment	✓		

WWW.ROSSSTORES.COM

OWINGS MILLS—9616 REISTERSTOWN RD (AT VALLEY CTR); 410.363.8001; M-SA 9:30-9:30, SU 11-7; PARKING LOT

Target

"...our favorite place to shop for kids' stuff—good selection and very affordable... guilt-free shopping—kids grow so fast so I don't want to pay high department-store prices... everything from diapers and sippy cups to car seats and strollers... easy return policy... generally helpful staff, but you don't go for the service—you go for the prices... decent registry that won't freak your friends out with outrageous prices... easy, convenient shopping for well-priced items... all the big-box brands available—Graco, Evenflo, Eddie Bauer, etc...."

Furniture, Bedding & Decor	✓	$$	Prices
Gear & Equipment	✓	4	Product availability
Nursing & Feeding	✓	3	Staff knowledge
Safety & Babycare	✓	3	Customer service
Clothing, Shoes & Accessories	✓	3	Decor
Books, Toys & Entertainment	✓		

WWW.TARGET.COM

OWINGS MILLS—11200 REISTERSTOWN RD (AT OWINGS MILLS BLVD); 410.654.9800; M-SA 8-10, SU 8-9; PARKING LOT

PIKESVILLE—1737 REISTERSTOWN RD (AT I 695); 410.486.4141; M-SA 8-10, SU 8-9; PARKING LOT

Tot Spot, The

"...a well-tended consignment shop... equipment, strollers, clothes, toys, books... truly gently used... they will pay cash for your used good, but they are quite choosey which is why you can always find something nice in their selection..."

Furniture, Bedding & Decor	✓	$	Prices
Gear & Equipment	✓	4	Product availability
Nursing & Feeding	✓	5	Staff knowledge
Safety & Babycare	✗	5	Customer service
Clothing, Shoes & Accessories	✓	4	Decor
Books, Toys & Entertainment	✓		

WWW.THETOTSPOTONLINE.COM

OWINGS MILLS—10811 REISTERSTOWN RD (NEAR ELEMENTARY SCHOOL); 410.654.1147; T-F10-6, SA 10-4, SU 12-5; FREE PARKING

Toys R Us

"...not just toys, but also tons of gear and supplies including diapers and formula... a hectic shopping experience but the prices make it all worthwhile... I've experienced good and bad service at the same store on the same day... the stores are huge and can be overwhelming...

most big brand-names available... leave the kids at home unless you want to end up with a cart full of toys... **"**

Furniture, Bedding & Decor......... ✓
Gear & Equipment....................... ✓
Nursing & Feeding .... ✓
Safety & Babycare....................... ✓
Clothing, Shoes & Accessories...... ✓
Books, Toys & Entertainment........ ✓

$$$.. Prices
❹ .... Product availability
❸ .... Staff knowledge
❸ ....Customer service
❸ .... Decor

WWW.TOYSRUS.COM

CATONSVILLE—6600 BALTIMORE NATIONAL PIKE (AT NUWOOD DR); 410.788.6678; M-SA 10-9 SU 11-6; PARKING LOT

OWINGS MILLS—10200 REISTERSTOWN RD (AT PAINTERS MILL RD); 410.356.4824; M-SA 10-9, SU 10-6; PARKING LOT

Value City

"*...if you are looking for bargain merchandise for the whole family, you'll find it here... you can always find something and lots of inexpensive baby and toddler clothes... very low prices with many sizes... chaotic atmosphere and hard to find staff, once you do they are very helpful... lines can be long...* **"**

Furniture, Bedding & Decor......... ✓
Gear & Equipment....................... ✓
Nursing & Feeding .... ✓
Safety & Babycare....................... ✓
Clothing, Shoes & Accessories...... ✓
Books, Toys & Entertainment........ ✓

$$.. Prices
❸ .... Product availability
❸ .... Staff knowledge
❸ ....Customer service
❸ .... Decor

WWW.VALUECITY.COM

CATONSVILLE—5840 BALTIMORE NATIONAL PIKE (AT INGLESIDE AVE); 410.788.2600; M-SA 10-9:30, SU 11-7

South of Baltimore

"lila picks"

★Be Beep
★Nordstrom
★Pottery Barn Kids
★The Right Start

Anne Arundel Medical Center Gift Shop

"...located in the garden lobby, this shop is clutch to last minute new baby gifts... they carry a nice selection, including preemie outfits... superb staff that is patient and actually seems to enjoy helping customers... lots to choose from..."

Furniture, Bedding & Decor	✗	$$$	Prices
Gear & Equipment	✗	❹	Product availability
Nursing & Feeding	✗	❹	Staff knowledge
Safety & Babycare	✗	❹	Customer service
Clothing, Shoes & Accessories	✓	❹	Decor
Books, Toys & Entertainment	✓		

WWW.AAHS.ORG

ANNAPOLIS—2001 MEDICAL PKWY (AT W ST); 443.481.5060; M-TH 9-7, F 9-4, SA 11-4; PARKING LOT

April Cornell

★★★½☆

"...beautiful, classic dresses and accessories for special occasions... I love the matching 'mommy and me' outfits... lots of fun knickknacks for sale... great selection of baby wear on their web site... rest assured your baby won't look like every other child in these adorable outfits... very frilly and girlie—beautiful..."

Furniture, Bedding & Decor	✗	$$$	Prices
Gear & Equipment	✗	❸	Product availability
Nursing & Feeding	✗	❹	Staff knowledge
Safety & Babycare	✗	❹	Customer service
Clothing, Shoes & Accessories	✓	❹	Decor
Books, Toys & Entertainment	✗		

ANNAPOLIS—16 MARKETSPLACE (AT MAIN ST); 410.263.4532; M-SA 10-6, SU 11-6

Babies R Us

"...everything baby under one roof... they have a wide selection and carry most 'mainstream' items such as Graco, Fisher-Price, Avent and Britax... great customer service—given how big the stores are, I was pleasantly surprised at how attentive the staff was... easy return policy... super busy on weekends so try to visit on a weekday for the best service... keep an eye out for great coupons, deals and frequent sales... easy and comprehensive registry... shopping here is so easy—you've got to check it out..."

Furniture, Bedding & Decor	✓	$$$	Prices
Gear & Equipment	✓	❹	Product availability

Nursing & Feeding	✓	❹	Staff knowledge
Safety & Babycare	✓	❹	Customer service
Clothing, Shoes & Accessories	✓	❹	Decor
Books, Toys & Entertainment	✓		

WWW.BABIESRUS.COM

PASADENA—8100 RITCHIE HWY (AT JUNIPERS HOLE RD); 410.863.8840; M-SA 9:30-9:30, SU 11-7:30; PARKING IN FRONT OF BLDG

Baby Depot At Burlington Coat Factory ★★★½☆

"...a large, 'super store' layout with a ton of baby gear... wide aisles, packed shelves, barely existent customer service and awesome prices... everything from bottles, car seats and strollers to gliders, cribs and clothes... I always find something worth getting... a little disorganized and hard to locate items you're looking for... the staff is not always knowledgeable about their merchandise... return policy is store credit only..."

Furniture, Bedding & Decor	✓	$$	Prices
Gear & Equipment	✓	❸	Product availability
Nursing & Feeding	✓	❸	Staff knowledge
Safety & Babycare	✓	❸	Customer service
Clothing, Shoes & Accessories	✓	❸	Decor
Books, Toys & Entertainment	✓		

WWW.BABYDEPOT.COM

ANNAPOLIS—158 DEFENSE HWY (AT HOUSLEY RD); 410.571.6818; M-SA 10-9, SU 11-6; PARKING LOT

ANNAPOLIS—2639 HOUSLEY RD (AT HIGHWAY 450); 410.571.6818; M-SA 10-9, SU 11-6; PARKING LOT

HANOVER—7000 ARUNDEL MILLS CIR (AT ARUNDEL MILLS MALL); 410.799.7450; M-SA 10-9:30, SU 11-7

BabyGap/GapKids ★★★★☆

"...colorful baby and toddler clothing in clean, well-lit stores... great return policy... it's the Gap, so you know what you're getting—colorful, cute and well-made clothing... best place for baby hats... prices are reasonable especially since there's always a sale of some sort going on... sales, sales, sales—frequent and fantastic... everything I'm looking for in infant clothing—snap crotches, snaps up the front, all natural fabrics and great styling... fun seasonal selections—a great place to shop for gifts as well as for your own kids... although it can get busy, staff generally seem accommodating and helpful..."

Furniture, Bedding & Decor	×	$$$	Prices
Gear & Equipment	×	❹	Product availability
Nursing & Feeding	×	❹	Staff knowledge
Safety & Babycare	×	❹	Customer service
Clothing, Shoes & Accessories	✓	❹	Decor
Books, Toys & Entertainment	×		

WWW.GAP.COM

ANNAPOLIS—43 ANNAPOLIS MALL (AT ANNAPOLIS MALL); 410.266.9616; M-SA 10-9:30, SU 11-6; MALL PARKING

Be Beep ★★★★★

"...my all time favorite toy and book store... play area for your toddlers while you shop... very unique selections plus something for everybody—even the child you think has everything... very kid friendly... high-end toy store with a ton of imagination and creativity based toys... I highly recommend to anyone looking for a better play experience for the child... a nice alternative to the chains..."

Furniture, Bedding & Decor	×	$$$$	Prices
Gear & Equipment	×	❹	Product availability
Nursing & Feeding	×	❹	Staff knowledge

Safety & Babycare .... ✗
Clothing, Shoes & Accessories....... ✓
Books, Toys & Entertainment .... ✓

❺ .... Customer service
❹ .... Decor

WWW.BEBEEPATOYSHOP.COM

ANNAPOLIS—2327C FOREST DR (AT RIVA RD); 410.224.4066; M-F 10-9, SA 10-6, SU 11-5

SEVERNA PARK—558A RITCHIE HWY (AT MCKINSEY RD); 410.544.1844; M-F 10-9, SA 10-6, SU 11-5

Bombay Kids ★★★★☆

"...the kids section of this furniture store carries out-of-the-ordinary items... whimsical, pastel grandfather clocks... zebra bean bags... perfect for my eclectic taste... I now prefer my daughter's room to my own... clean bathroom with changing area and wipes... they have a little table with crayons and coloring books for the kids... easy and relaxed shopping destination..."

Furniture, Bedding & Decor .... ✓
Gear & Equipment .... ✗
Nursing & Feeding........................ ✗
Safety & Babycare .... ✗
Clothing, Shoes & Accessories....... ✗
Books, Toys & Entertainment .... ✗

$$$ .... Prices
❹ .... Product availability
❹ .... Staff knowledge
❹ .... Customer service
❹ .... Decor

WWW.BOMBAYKIDS.COM

ANNAPOLIS—2337 A & 2341 G FOREST DR (AT FOREST DR); 410.266.9670; M-SA 10-9 11-6 SU; PARKING LOT

Carter's ★★★★☆

"...always a great selection of inexpensive baby basics—everything from clothing to linens... I always find something at 'giveaway prices' during one of their frequent sales... busy and crowded—it can be a chaotic shopping experience... 30 to 50 percent less than what you would pay at other boutiques... I bought five pieces of baby clothing for less than $40... durable, adorable and affordable... most stores have a small play area for kids in center of store so you can get your shopping done..."

Furniture, Bedding & Decor .... ✓
Gear & Equipment .... ✗
Nursing & Feeding........................ ✗
Safety & Babycare .... ✗
Clothing, Shoes & Accessories....... ✓
Books, Toys & Entertainment .... ✓

$$ .... Prices
❹ .... Product availability
❹ .... Staff knowledge
❹ .... Customer service
❹ .... Decor

WWW.CARTERS.COM

HANOVER—7000 ARUNDEL MILLS CIR (AT ARUNDEL MILLS); 443.755.8950; M-SA 10-9:30 SU 11-7; FREE PARKING

Children's Place, The ★★★½☆

"...great bargains on cute clothing... shoes, socks, swimsuits, sunglasses and everything in between... lots of '3 for $20' type deals on sleepers, pants and mix-and-match separates... so much more affordable than the other 'big chains'... don't expect the most unique stuff here, but it wears and washes well... cheap clothing for cheap prices... you can leave the store with bags full of clothes without putting a huge dent in your wallet..."

Furniture, Bedding & Decor .... ✗
Gear & Equipment .... ✗
Nursing & Feeding........................ ✗
Safety & Babycare .... ✗
Clothing, Shoes & Accessories....... ✓
Books, Toys & Entertainment .... ✓

$$ .... Prices
❹ .... Product availability
❹ .... Staff knowledge
❹ .... Customer service
❹ .... Decor

WWW.CHILDRENSPLACE.COM

HANOVER—7000 ARUNDEL MILLS CIR (AT RIDGE RD); 443.755.1525; M-SA 10-9:30, SU 11-7; PARKING LOT

Costco

"...dependable place for bulk diapers, wipes and formula at discount prices... clothing selection is very hit-or-miss... avoid shopping there during nights and weekends if possible, because parking and checkout lines are brutal... they don't have a huge selection of brands, but the brands they do have are almost always in stock and at a great price... lowest prices around for diapers and formula... kid's clothing tends to be picked through, but it's worth looking for great deals on name-brand items like Carter's..."

Furniture, Bedding & Decor .... ✓ | $$ .... Prices
Gear & Equipment .... ✓ | ❸ .... Product availability
Nursing & Feeding .... ✓ | ❸ .... Staff knowledge
Safety & Babycare .... ✓ | ❸ .... Customer service
Clothing, Shoes & Accessories .... ✓ | ❷ .... Decor
Books, Toys & Entertainment .... ✓

WWW.COSTCO.COM

GLEN BURNIE—575 E ORDNANCE RD (AT RT 710); 410.590.8603; M-F 11-8:30, SA 9:30-6, SU 10-6

Giant Peach

Furniture, Bedding & Decor .... ✗ | ✗ .... Gear & Equipment
Nursing & Feeding .... ✗ | ✗ .... Safety & Babycare
Clothing, Shoes & Accessories .... ✓ | ✗ .... Books, Toys & Entertainment

ANNAPOLIS—17 ANNAPOLIS ST (OFF ROWE BLVD); 410.268.8776; M-SA 10-5:30

Gymboree

"...beautiful clothing and great quality... colorful and stylish baby and kids wear... lots of fun birthday gift ideas... easy exchange and return policy... items usually go on sale pretty quickly... save money with Gymbucks... many stores have a play area which makes shopping with my kids fun (let alone feasible)..."

Furniture, Bedding & Decor .... ✗ | $$$ .... Prices
Gear & Equipment .... ✗ | ❹ .... Product availability
Nursing & Feeding .... ✗ | ❹ .... Staff knowledge
Safety & Babycare .... ✗ | ❹ .... Customer service
Clothing, Shoes & Accessories .... ✓ | ❹ .... Decor
Books, Toys & Entertainment .... ✓

WWW.GYMBOREE.COM

ANNAPOLIS—53 ANNAPOLIS MALL (AT ANNAPOLIS MALL); 410.224.6968; M-SA 10-9, SU 11-6; MALL PARKING

H & M

"...wonderful prices for trendy baby and toddler clothes... it's the 'Euro' Target... buy for yourself and for your kids... a fun shopping experience as long as your child doesn't mind the bright lights and loud music... decent return policy... incredible sale prices... store can get messy at peak hours... busy and hectic, but their inventory is fun and worth the visit..."

Furniture, Bedding & Decor .... ✗ | $$ .... Prices
Gear & Equipment .... ✗ | ❸ .... Product availability
Nursing & Feeding .... ✗ | ❸ .... Staff knowledge
Safety & Babycare .... ✗ | ❸ .... Customer service
Clothing, Shoes & Accessories .... ✓ | ❸ .... Decor
Books, Toys & Entertainment .... ✓

WWW.HM.COM

HANOVER—7000 ARUNDEL MILLS CIR (AT ARUNDEL MILLS CTR); 410.799.0824; M-SA 10-9:30, SU 11-7; PARKING LOT

Hecht's

"...the baby department at Hecht's has a nice selection of moderately priced items... especially good selection for girl's clothes... the prices are right, but the service can be spotty... large and impersonal, messy racks, lack of service and style... pretty much your basic department store... good for baby gifts like picture frames and scrap books..."

Furniture, Bedding & Decor	✗	$$$	Prices
Gear & Equipment	✗	❸	Product availability
Nursing & Feeding	✗	❸	Staff knowledge
Safety & Babycare	✗	❸	Customer service
Clothing, Shoes & Accessories	✓	❸	Decor
Books, Toys & Entertainment	✓		

WWW.HECHTS.COM

ANNAPOLIS—1295 ANNAPOLIS MALL (AT RT 50 & 450); 410.266.0800; CHECK SCHEDULE ONLINE; MALL PARKING

GLEN BURNIE—7900 RICHIE HWY (AT MARLEY STATION MALL); 410.766.2055; CHECK SCHEDULE ONLINE; MALL PARKING

JCPenney

"...always a good place to find clothes and other baby basics... the registry process was seamless... staff is generally friendly but the lines always seem long and slow... they don't have the greatest selection of toddler clothes, but their baby section is great... we had some damaged furniture delivered but customer service was easy and accommodating... a pretty limited selection of gear, but what they have is priced right..."

Furniture, Bedding & Decor	✓	$$	Prices
Gear & Equipment	✓	❸	Product availability
Nursing & Feeding	✓	❸	Staff knowledge
Safety & Babycare	✓	❸	Customer service
Clothing, Shoes & Accessories	✓	❸	Decor
Books, Toys & Entertainment	✓		

WWW.JCPENNEY.COM

ANNAPOLIS—1695 ANNAPOLIS MALL (AT ANNAPOLIS MALL); 410.224.6500; M-SA 10-9:30, SU 11-6; PARKING LOT

GLEN BURNIE—7900 RITCHIE HWY (AT MARLEY STATION SHOPPING CTR); 410.760.7724; M-SA 10-9:30, SU 11-6; PARKING LOT

Joan's Hallmark

"...birth announcements... baby books... gifts for new and expected babies (plus their parents)... a well laid out store... friendly service..."

Furniture, Bedding & Decor	✗	$$	Prices
Gear & Equipment	✗	❹	Product availability
Nursing & Feeding	✗	❹	Staff knowledge
Safety & Babycare	✗	❺	Customer service
Clothing, Shoes & Accessories	✗	❺	Decor
Books, Toys & Entertainment	✗		

WWW.HALLMARK.COM

ANNAPOLIS—2327-B FOREST DR (AT RTE 2); 410.266.8508; M-F 10-8, SA 10-6, SU 11-5; FREE PARKING

KB Toys

"...hectic and always buzzing... wall-to-wall plastic and blinking lights... more Fisher-Price, Elmo and Sponge Bob than the eye can handle... a toy super store with discounted prices... they always have some kind of special sale going on... if you're looking for the latest and greatest popular toy, then look no further—not the place for unique or unusual toys... perfect for bulk toy shopping—especially around the holidays..."

Furniture, Bedding & Decor	✗	$$	Prices
Gear & Equipment	✗	❸	Product availability

Nursing & Feeding ✗	❸ Staff knowledge
Safety & Babycare ✗	❸ Customer service
Clothing, Shoes & Accessories ✗	❸ Decor
Books, Toys & Entertainment ✓	

WWW.KBTOYS.COM

GLEN BURNIE—GOV RITCHIE HWY,RTS 2&100 (AT MARLEY STATION); 410.760.9889; M-SA 10-9:30, SU 11-6

HANOVER—7600 CLARK RD (AT ARUNDEL MILLS MALL); 443.755.9824; M-SA 10-9:30, SU 11-7:30; MALL PARKING

Kohl's ★★★★☆

"...nice one-stop shopping for the whole family—everything from clothing to baby gear... great sales on clothing and a good selection of higher-end brands... stylish, inexpensive clothes for babies through 24 months... very easy shopping experience... dirt-cheap sales and clearance prices... nothing super fancy, but just right for those everyday romper outfits... Graco, Eddie Bauer and other well-known brands..."

Furniture, Bedding & Decor ✓	$$ Prices
Gear & Equipment ✓	❹ Product availability
Nursing & Feeding ✓	❸ Staff knowledge
Safety & Babycare ✓	❸ Customer service
Clothing, Shoes & Accessories ✓	❸ Decor
Books, Toys & Entertainment ✓	

WWW.KOHLS.COM

SEVERNA PARK—575 RITCHIE HWY (AT ROBINSON RD); 410.544.6993; M-SA 8-10, SU 10-8

Macy's ★★★½☆

"...Macy's has it all and I never leave empty-handed... if you time your visit right you can find some great deals... go during the week so you don't get overwhelmed with the weekend crowd... good for staples as well as beautiful party dresses for girls... lots of brand-names like Carter's, Guess, and Ralph Lauren... not much in terms of assistance... newspaper coupons and sales help keep the cost down... some stores are better organized and maintained than others... if you're going to shop at a department store for your baby, then Macy's is a safe bet..."

Furniture, Bedding & Decor ✓	$$$ Prices
Gear & Equipment ✗	❸ Product availability
Nursing & Feeding ✗	❸ Staff knowledge
Safety & Babycare ✗	❸ Customer service
Clothing, Shoes & Accessories ✓	❸ Decor
Books, Toys & Entertainment ✓	

WWW.MACYS.COM

GLEN BURNIE—7900 RITCHIE HWY (AT MARLEY STATION SHOPPING CTR); 410.760.2100; M-F 10-9, SA 10-9:30, SU 11-6; PARKING LOT

Nordstrom ★★★★★

"...quality service and quality clothes... awesome kids shoe department—almost as good as the one for adults... free balloons in the children's shoe area as well as drawing tables... in addition to their own brand, they carry a very nice selection of other high-end baby clothing including Ralph Lauren, Robeez, etc... adorable baby clothes—they make great shower gifts... such a wonderful shopping experience—their lounge is perfect for breastfeeding and for changing diapers... well-rounded selection of baby basics as well as fancy clothes for special events..."

Furniture, Bedding & Decor ✓	$$$$ Prices
Gear & Equipment ✓	❹ Product availability
Nursing & Feeding ✗	❹ Staff knowledge
Safety & Babycare ✗	❹ Customer service
Clothing, Shoes & Accessories ✓	❹ Decor

Books, Toys & Entertainment .... ✓

WWW.NORDSTROM.COM

ANNAPOLIS—20 ANNAPOLIS MALL (OFF JENNIFER RD); 410.573.1121; M-SA 10-9:30 SU 11-6; PARKING LOT

Old Navy

"...hip and 'in' clothes for infants and tots... plenty of steals on clearance items... T-shirts and pants for $10 or less... busy, busy, busy long lines, especially on weekends... nothing fancy and you won't mind when your kids get down and dirty in these clothes... easy to wash, decent quality... you can shop for your baby, your toddler, your teen and yourself all at the same time... clothes are especially affordable when you hit their sales (post-holiday sales are amazing!)..."

Furniture, Bedding & Decor	✗	$$	Prices
Gear & Equipment	✗	❹	Product availability
Nursing & Feeding	✗	❸	Staff knowledge
Safety & Babycare	✗	❸	Customer service
Clothing, Shoes & Accessories	✓	❸	Decor
Books, Toys & Entertainment	✗		

WWW.OLDNAVY.COM

ANNAPOLIS—2532 SOLOMONS ISLAND RD (AT ARIS T ALLEN BLVD); 410.573.9110; M-SA 9-9, SU 10-6; PARKING LOT

HANOVER—7000 ARUNDEL MILLS CIR (AT ARUNDEL MILLS MALL); 443.755.0416; M-SA 10-9:30, SU 11-7; MALL PARKING

SEVERNA PARK—571 RITCHIE HWY (AT MCKINSEY RD); 410.384.9267; M-SA 9-9, SU 11-6; PARKING LOT

OshKosh B'Gosh

"...cute, sturdy clothes for infants and toddlers... frequent sales make their high-quality merchandise a lot more affordable... doesn't every American kid have to get a pair of their overalls?.. great selection of cute clothes for boys... you can't go wrong here—their clothing is fun and worth the price... customer service is pretty hit-or-miss from store to store... we always walk out of here with something fun and colorful..."

Furniture, Bedding & Decor	✗	$$$	Prices
Gear & Equipment	✗	❹	Product availability
Nursing & Feeding	✗	❹	Staff knowledge
Safety & Babycare	✗	❹	Customer service
Clothing, Shoes & Accessories	✓	❹	Decor
Books, Toys & Entertainment	✗		

WWW.OSHKOSHBGOSH.COM

HANOVER—7000 ARUNDEL MILLS CIR (AT ARUNDEL MILLS MALL); 443.755.1701; M-SA 10-9:30, SU 11-7; MALL PARKING

Pier 1 Kids

"...everything from curtains and dressers to teddy bears and piggy banks... attractive furniture and prices are moderate to expensive... staff provided lots of help assembling a 'look' for my child's room... we had an excellent shopping experience here... the salesperson told my kids it was okay to touch everything because it's all kid friendly... takes you out of the crib stage and into the next step..."

Furniture, Bedding & Decor	✓	$$$	Prices
Gear & Equipment	✗	❸	Product availability
Nursing & Feeding	✗	❹	Staff knowledge
Safety & Babycare	✗	❹	Customer service
Clothing, Shoes & Accessories	✗	❹	Decor
Books, Toys & Entertainment	✗		

WWW.PIER1KIDS.COM

HANOVER—7651 ARUNDEL MILLS BLVD ST 3 (AT MILFORD AVE); 443.755.9220; M-SA 10-9 SU 11-7

Pottery Barn Kids

"...stylish furniture, rugs, rockers and much more... they've found the right mix between quality and price... finally a company that stands behind what they sell—their customer service is great... gorgeous baby decor and furniture that will make your nursery to-die-for... the play area is so much fun—my daughter never wants to leave... a beautiful store with tons of ideas for setting up your nursery or kid's room... bright colors and cute patterns with basics to mix and match... if you see something in the catalog, but not in the store, just ask because they often have it in the back..."

Furniture, Bedding & Decor	✓	$$$$	Prices
Gear & Equipment	✗	❹	Product availability
Nursing & Feeding	✗	❹	Staff knowledge
Safety & Babycare	✗	❹	Customer service
Clothing, Shoes & Accessories	✗	❺	Decor
Books, Toys & Entertainment	✓		

WWW.POTTERYBARNKIDS.COM

ANNAPOLIS—2002 ANNAPOLIS MALL (AT ANNAPOLIS MALL); 410.897.9824; M-SA 10-9:30, SU 11-6; MALL PARKING

Rainbow Kids

"...fun clothing styles for infants and tots at low prices... the quality isn't the same as the more expensive brands, but the sleepers and play outfits always hold up well... qreat place for basics... cute trendy shoe selection for your little walker... we love the prices... up-to-date selection..."

Furniture, Bedding & Decor	✗	$$	Prices
Gear & Equipment	✓	❸	Product availability
Nursing & Feeding	✗	❸	Staff knowledge
Safety & Babycare	✗	❸	Customer service
Clothing, Shoes & Accessories	✓	❸	Decor
Books, Toys & Entertainment	✓		

WWW.RAINBOWSHOPS.COM

GLEN BURNIE—6711 RITCHIE HWY (AT GLEN BURNIE MALL); 410.590.2541; M-SA 10-9, SU 11-6; PARKING LOT

Return To Oz

Furniture, Bedding & Decor	✗	✗	Gear & Equipment
Nursing & Feeding	✗	✗	Safety & Babycare
Clothing, Shoes & Accessories	✓	✗	Books, Toys & Entertainment

ANNAPOLIS—45 OLD SOLOMONS ISLAND; 410.266.9390; DAILY 10-5

Right Start, The

"...higher-end, well selected items... Britax, Maclaren, Combi, Mustela—all the cool brands under one roof... everything from bibs to bottles and even the Bugaboo stroller... prices seem a little high, but the selection is good and the staff knowledgeable and helpful... there are toys all over the store that kids can play with while you shop... I have a hard time getting my kids out of the store because they are having so much fun... a boutique-like shopping experience but they carry most of the key brands... their registry works well..."

Furniture, Bedding & Decor	✓	$$$	Prices
Gear & Equipment	✓	❹	Product availability
Nursing & Feeding	✓	❹	Staff knowledge
Safety & Babycare	✓	❹	Customer service
Clothing, Shoes & Accessories	✓	❹	Decor
Books, Toys & Entertainment	✓		

WWW.RIGHTSTART.COM

ANNAPOLIS—1365 ANNAPOLIS MALL (AT ANNAPOLIS MALL); 410.571.9003; M-SA 10-9, SU 11-6; MALL PARKING

Sears

"...a decent selection of clothes and basic baby equipment... check out the Kids Club program—it's a great way to save money... you go to Sears to save money, not to be pampered... the quality of their merchandise is better than Wal-Mart, but don't expect anything too special or different... not much in terms of gear, but tons of well priced baby and toddler clothing..."

Furniture, Bedding & Decor	✓	$$	Prices
Gear & Equipment	✓	❸	Product availability
Nursing & Feeding	✓	❸	Staff knowledge
Safety & Babycare	✓	❸	Customer service
Clothing, Shoes & Accessories	✓	❸	Decor
Books, Toys & Entertainment	✓		

WWW.SEARS.COM

ANNAPOLIS—1040 ANNAPOLIS MALL (AT JENNIFER RD); 443.926.5200; M-F 10-9, SA 10-6, SU 11-5; PARKING LOT

GLEN BURNIE—7900 GOV RITCHIE HWY (AT MARLEY STATION RD); 410.590.2400; M-F 9:30-9:30, SA 8-9:30, SU 11-7

Stride Rite Shoes

"...wonderful selection of baby and toddler shoes... sandals, sneakers, and even special-occasion shoes... decent quality shoes that last... they know a lot about kids' shoes and take the time to get it right—they always measure my son's feet before fittings... store sizes vary, but they always have something in stock that works... they've even special ordered shoes for my daughter... a fun 'first shoe' buying experience..."

Furniture, Bedding & Decor	✗	$$$	Prices
Gear & Equipment	✗	❹	Product availability
Nursing & Feeding	✗	❹	Staff knowledge
Safety & Babycare	✗	❹	Customer service
Clothing, Shoes & Accessories	✓	❹	Decor
Books, Toys & Entertainment	✗		

WWW.STRIDERITE.COM

ANNAPOLIS—120 ANNAPOLIS MALL (AT ANNAPOLIS MALL); 410.266.3003; M-SA 10-9:30, SU 11-6

GLEN BURNIE—C-127-7900 GOV RICHIE HWY (AT MARLA STATION MALL); 410.768.4193; M-SA 10-9:30, SU 11-6; PARKING LOT

Target

"...our favorite place to shop for kids' stuff—good selection and very affordable... guilt-free shopping—kids grow so fast so I don't want to pay high department-store prices... everything from diapers and sippy cups to car seats and strollers... easy return policy... generally helpful staff, but you don't go for the service you go for the prices... decent registry that won't freak your friends out with outrageous prices... easy, convenient shopping for well-priced items... all the big-box brands available—Graco, Evenflo, Eddie Bauer, etc...."

Furniture, Bedding & Decor	✓	$$	Prices
Gear & Equipment	✓	❹	Product availability
Nursing & Feeding	✓	❸	Staff knowledge
Safety & Babycare	✓	❸	Customer service
Clothing, Shoes & Accessories	✓	❸	Decor
Books, Toys & Entertainment	✓		

WWW.TARGET.COM

GLEN BURNIE—7951 NOLPARK CT (AT NOLPARK RD); 410.969.2257; M-SA 8-10, SU 8-9; PARKING IN FRONT OF BLDG

Toys R Us

"...not just toys, but also tons of gear and supplies including diapers and formula... a hectic shopping experience but the prices make it all worthwhile... I've experienced good and bad service at the same store on the same day... the stores are huge and can be overwhelming... most big brand-names available... leave the kids at home unless you want to end up with a cart full of toys..."

Furniture, Bedding & Decor	✓	$$$	Prices
Gear & Equipment	✓	❹	Product availability
Nursing & Feeding	✓	❸	Staff knowledge
Safety & Babycare	✓	❸	Customer service
Clothing, Shoes & Accessories	✓	❸	Decor
Books, Toys & Entertainment	✓		

WWW.TOYSRUS.COM

ANNAPOLIS—41 DEFENSE HWY (AT SPRUCE LN); 410.573.0440; M-SA 10-9, SU 10-6; PARKING LOT

GLEN BURNIE—6711 RITCHIE HWY (AT GLEN BURNIE MALL); 410.768.4050; M-SA 10-9, SU 10-6; MALL PARKING

Value City

"...if you are looking for bargain merchandise for the whole family, you'll find it here... you can always find something and lots of inexpensive baby and toddler clothes... very low prices with many sizes... chaotic atmosphere and hard to find staff, once you do they are very helpful... lines can be long..."

Furniture, Bedding & Decor	✓	$$	Prices
Gear & Equipment	✓	❸	Product availability
Nursing & Feeding	✓	❸	Staff knowledge
Safety & Babycare	✓	❸	Customer service
Clothing, Shoes & Accessories	✓	❸	Decor
Books, Toys & Entertainment	✓		

WWW.VALUECITY.COM

GLEN BURNIE—7700 RITCHIE HWY (AT BERRY RD); 410.553.6500; M-TH 10-9 F-SA 10-9:30 SU 11-7; PARKING LOT

East of Baltimore

"lila picks"

★IKEA

Hecht's

"...the baby department at Hecht's has a nice selection of moderately priced items... especially good selection for girl's clothes... the prices are right, but the service can be spotty... large and impersonal, messy racks, lack of service and style... pretty much your basic department store... good for baby gifts like picture frames and scrap books..."

Furniture, Bedding & Decor	✗	$$$	Prices
Gear & Equipment	✗	❸	Product availability
Nursing & Feeding	✗	❸	Staff knowledge
Safety & Babycare	✗	❸	Customer service
Clothing, Shoes & Accessories	✓	❸	Decor
Books, Toys & Entertainment	✓		

WWW.HECHTS.COM

WHITE MARSH—8200 PERRY HALL BLVD (AT WHITE MARSH MALL); 410.931.2000; CHECK SCHEDULE ONLINE

IKEA

"...the coolest-looking and best-priced bedding, bibs and eating utensils in town... fun, practical style and the prices are definitely right... one of the few stores around that lets kids climb and crawl on furniture... the kids' area has a slide, tunnels, tents... is it an indoor playground or a store?.. unending decorating ideas for families on a budget (lamps, rugs, beds, bedding)... it's all about organization—cubbies, drawers, shelves, seats that double as a trunk and step stool... arts and crafts galore... free childcare while you shop... cheap eats if you get hungry..."

Furniture, Bedding & Decor	✓	$$	Prices
Gear & Equipment	✗	❹	Product availability
Nursing & Feeding	✓	❹	Staff knowledge
Safety & Babycare	✓	❹	Customer service
Clothing, Shoes & Accessories	✗	❹	Decor
Books, Toys & Entertainment	✓		

WWW.IKEA.COM

WHITE MARSH—8352 HONEYGO BLVD (AT WHITE MARSH BLVD); 410.931.5400; M-F 10-9, SA 9-9, SU 10-8

JCPenney

"...always a good place to find clothes and other baby basics... the registry process was seamless... staff is generally friendly but the lines always seem long and slow... they don't have the greatest selection of toddler clothes, but their baby section is great... we had some damaged furniture delivered but customer service was easy and accommodating... a pretty limited selection of gear, but what they have is priced right..."

Furniture, Bedding & Decor ✓	$$ Prices
Gear & Equipment ✓	❸ Product availability
Nursing & Feeding ✓	❸ Staff knowledge
Safety & Babycare ✓	❸ Customer service
Clothing, Shoes & Accessories ✓	❸ Decor
Books, Toys & Entertainment ✓	

WWW.JCPENNEY.COM

WHITE MARSH—8200 PERRY HALL BLVD (AT WHITE MARSH MALL); 410.931.7550; M-TH 10-9:30, F 10-10, SA 9-10, SU 11-7; PARKING LOT

Macy's ★★★½☆

"...Macy's has it all and I never leave empty-handed... if you time your visit right you can find some great deals... go during the week so you don't get overwhelmed with the weekend crowd... good for staples as well as beautiful party dresses for girls... lots of brand-names like Carter's, Guess, and Ralph Lauren... not much in terms of assistance... newspaper coupons and sales help keep the cost down... some stores are better organized and maintained than others... if you're going to shop at a department store for your baby, then Macy's is a safe bet..."

Furniture, Bedding & Decor ✓	$$$ Prices
Gear & Equipment ✗	❸ Product availability
Nursing & Feeding ✗	❸ Staff knowledge
Safety & Babycare ✗	❸ Customer service
Clothing, Shoes & Accessories ✓	❸ Decor
Books, Toys & Entertainment ✓	

WWW.MACYS.COM

PERRY HALL—8200 PERRY HALL BLVD (AT WHITE MARSH MALL); 410.931.7000; M-SA 10-9:30, SU 11-6; PARKING LOT

Old Navy ★★★★☆

"...hip and 'in' clothes for infants and tots... plenty of steals on clearance items... T-shirts and pants for $10 or less... busy, busy, busy—long lines, especially on weekends... nothing fancy and you won't mind when your kids get down and dirty in these clothes... easy to wash, decent quality... you can shop for your baby, your toddler, your teen and yourself all at the same time... clothes are especially affordable when you hit their sales (post-holiday sales are amazing!)..."

Furniture, Bedding & Decor ✗	$$ Prices
Gear & Equipment ✗	❹ Product availability
Nursing & Feeding ✗	❸ Staff knowledge
Safety & Babycare ✗	❸ Customer service
Clothing, Shoes & Accessories ✓	❸ Decor
Books, Toys & Entertainment ✗	

WWW.OLDNAVY.COM

WHITE MARSH—8123 HONEYGO BLVD (AT WHITE MARSH MALL); 410.933.3650; M-SA 9-9, SU 10-6; MALL PARKING

Online

"lila picks"

★babycenter.com ★babystyle.com

★babyuniverse.com ★joggingstroller.com

ababy.com

Furniture, Bedding & Decor ✓ ✓ Gear & Equipment
Nursing & Feeding ✗ ✓ Safety & Babycare
Clothing, Shoes & Accessories ✓ ✗ Books, Toys & Entertainment

aikobaby.com ★★★☆☆

"...high end clothes that are so cute... everything from Catamini to Jack and Lily... you can find super expensive infant and baby clothes at discounted prices... amazing selection of diaper bags so you don't have to look like a frumpy mom (or dad)..."

Furniture, Bedding & Decor ✗ ✓ Gear & Equipment
Nursing & Feeding ✗ ✗ Safety & Babycare
Clothing, Shoes & Accessories ✓ ✗ Books, Toys & Entertainment

albeebaby.com ★★★★☆

"...they offer a really comprehensive selection of baby gear... their prices are some of the best online... great discounts on Maclarens before the new models come out... good product availability—fast shipping and easy transactions... the site is pretty easy to use... the prices are surprisingly great..."

Furniture, Bedding & Decor ✓ ✓ Gear & Equipment
Nursing & Feeding ✓ ✓ Safety & Babycare
Clothing, Shoes & Accessories ✓ ✓ Books, Toys & Entertainment

amazon.com ★★★★½

"...unless you've been living under a rock, you know that in addition to books, Amazon carries an amazing amount of baby stuff too... they have the best prices and offer free shipping on bigger purchases... you can even buy used items for dirt cheap... I always read the comments written by others—they're very useful in helping make my decisions... I love Amazon for just about everything, but their baby selection only carries the big box standards..."

Furniture, Bedding & Decor ✗ ✓ Gear & Equipment
Nursing & Feeding ✓ ✓ Safety & Babycare
Clothing, Shoes & Accessories ✓ ✓ Books, Toys & Entertainment

arunningstroller.com ★★★★½

"...the prices are very competitive and the customer service is great... I talked to them on the phone for a while and they totally hooked me up with the right model... if you're looking for a new stroller, look no further... talk to Marilyn—she's the best... shipping costs are reasonable and their prices overall are good..."

Furniture, Bedding & Decor ✓ ✓ Gear & Equipment
Nursing & Feeding ✗ ✗ Safety & Babycare
Clothing, Shoes & Accessories ✗ ✗ Books, Toys & Entertainment

babiesinthesun.com ★★★★☆

"...one-stop shopping for cloth diapers... run by a fantastic woman who had 3 cloth diapered babies herself and is a wealth of knowledge... if you live in South Florida, the owner will let you into her home to see the merchandise and ask questions... great selection and the customer service is the best..."

Furniture, Bedding & Decor ✗ ✓ Gear & Equipment
Nursing & Feeding ✗ ✓ Safety & Babycare
Clothing, Shoes & Accessories ✗ ✗ Books, Toys & Entertainment

babiesrus.com ★★★★☆

"...terrific web site with all the baby gear you'll need... registering online made it easy for my family and friends... getting the registry activated was a bit tricky... super convenient and ideal for the moms-to-be who are on bedrest... web site prices are comparable to in-store prices... shipping is usually free... a very efficient way to buy and send baby gifts... our local Babies R Us said they will accept returns if they carry the same item... not all online items are available in your local store..."

Furniture, Bedding & Decor ✓ ✓ Gear & Equipment
Nursing & Feeding ✓ ✓ Safety & Babycare
Clothing, Shoes & Accessories ✓ ✓ Books, Toys & Entertainment

babiestravellite.com ★★★★½

"...caters to traveling families... they deliver baby items to your hotel room anywhere in the country... all of the different baby supplies you will need when you travel with a baby or a toddler... they sell almost every major brand for each product and their prices are sometimes cheaper than you would find at your local store..."

Furniture, Bedding & Decor ✗ ✗ Gear & Equipment
Nursing & Feeding ✓ ✓ Safety & Babycare
Clothing, Shoes & Accessories ✗ ✓ Books, Toys & Entertainment

babyage.com ★★★★☆

"...fast shipping and the best prices around... flat rate shipping is great after the baby has arrived and you don't have time to go to the store... very attentive customer service... clearance items are a great deal (regular items are very competitive too)... ordering and delivery were super smooth... I usually check this web site before I purchase any baby gear... sign up for their newsletter and they'll notify you when they are having a sale..."

Furniture, Bedding & Decor ✓ ✓ Gear & Equipment
Nursing & Feeding ✓ ✓ Safety & Babycare
Clothing, Shoes & Accessories ✓ ✓ Books, Toys & Entertainment

babyant.com ★★★★☆

"...wide variety of brands and products available through their site... super easy to navigate... fun, whimsical ideas... nice people and helpful... easy to return items and you can call them with questions... often has the best prices and low shipping costs..."

Furniture, Bedding & Decor ✓ ✓ Gear & Equipment
Nursing & Feeding ✓ ✓ Safety & Babycare
Clothing, Shoes & Accessories ✓ ✓ Books, Toys & Entertainment

babybazaar.com

"...high-end baby stuff available on an easy-to-use web site... lots of European styles... quick processing and shipping... mom's tips, educational toys, exclusive favorites Bugaboo and Stokke..."

Furniture, Bedding & Decor .... ✓ ✓ .... Gear & Equipment
Nursing & Feeding .... ✓ ✓ .... Safety & Babycare
Clothing, Shoes & Accessories .... ✓ ✓ .... Books, Toys & Entertainment

babybestbuy.com

Furniture, Bedding & Decor .... ✓ ✓ .... Gear & Equipment
Nursing & Feeding .... ✓ ✓ .... Safety & Babycare
Clothing, Shoes & Accessories .... ✓ ✓ .... Books, Toys & Entertainment

babycatalog.com ★★★★☆

"...great deals on many essentials... wide selection of rockers but fewer options in other categories... the web site could be more user-friendly... customer service and delivery was fast and efficient... check out their seasonal specials... the baby club is a great way to save additional money... sign up for their wonderful pregnancy/new baby email newsletter... check this web site before you buy anywhere else..."

Furniture, Bedding & Decor .... ✓ ✓ .... Gear & Equipment
Nursing & Feeding .... ✓ ✓ .... Safety & Babycare
Clothing, Shoes & Accessories .... ✓ ✓ .... Books, Toys & Entertainment

babycenter.com ★★★★★

"...a terrific selection of all things baby, plus quick shipping... free shipping on big orders... makes shopping convenient for new parents... web site is very user friendly... they always email you about sale items and special offers... lots of useful information for parents... carries everything you may need... online registry is simple, easy and a great way to get what you need... includes helpful products ratings by parents... they've created a nice online community in addition to their online store..."

Furniture, Bedding & Decor .... ✓ ✓ .... Gear & Equipment
Nursing & Feeding .... ✓ ✓ .... Safety & Babycare
Clothing, Shoes & Accessories .... ✓ ✓ .... Books, Toys & Entertainment

babydepot.com ★★★☆☆

"...carries everything you'll find in a big department store but at cheaper prices and with everything all in one place... be certain you know what you want because returns can be difficult... site could be more user-friendly... online selection can differ from instore selection... love the online registry..."

Furniture, Bedding & Decor .... ✓ ✓ .... Gear & Equipment
Nursing & Feeding .... ✓ ✓ .... Safety & Babycare
Clothing, Shoes & Accessories .... ✓ ✓ .... Books, Toys & Entertainment

babygeared.com

Furniture, Bedding & Decor .... ✓ ✓ .... Gear & Equipment
Nursing & Feeding .... ✓ ✓ .... Safety & Babycare
Clothing, Shoes & Accessories .... ✓ ✓ .... Books, Toys & Entertainment

babyphd.com

Furniture, Bedding & Decor .... ✓ ✗ .... Gear & Equipment
Nursing & Feeding .... ✗ ✗ .... Safety & Babycare
Clothing, Shoes & Accessories .... ✓ ✓ .... Books, Toys & Entertainment

babystyle.com ★★★★★

"...their web site is just like their stores—terrific... an excellent source for everything a parent needs... fantastic maternity and baby clothes...

they always respond quickly by email... their site seems to have even more merchandise than their stores... I started shopping on their site after receiving a gift card—very easy and convenient... wonderful selection... ”

Furniture, Bedding & Decor .... ✓ ✓ .... Gear & Equipment
Nursing & Feeding .... ✓ ✓ .... Safety & Babycare
Clothing, Shoes & Accessories ...... ✓ ✓ .... Books, Toys & Entertainment

babysupermall.com

Furniture, Bedding & Decor .... ✓ ✓ .... Gear & Equipment
Nursing & Feeding .... ✓ ✓ .... Safety & Babycare
Clothing, Shoes & Accessories ...... ✓ ✓ .... Books, Toys & Entertainment

babyuniverse.com ★★★★★

“*...nice large selection of specialty and basic items... easy-to-use web site with decent prices... carries Carter's clothes and many other popular brands... great bedding selection - they're one of the few places with the Kidsline bedding I wanted... adorable backpacks for toddlers and preschoolers... check out the site for strollers and car seats... this was my first online shopping experience and they made it so easy, convenient and fast, I was hooked... fine customer service... flat rate (if not free) shipping takes the 'ouch' factor out of those big ticket purchases...* ”

Furniture, Bedding & Decor .... ✓ ✓ .... Gear & Equipment
Nursing & Feeding .... ✓ ✓ .... Safety & Babycare
Clothing, Shoes & Accessories ...... ✓ ✓ .... Books, Toys & Entertainment

barebabies.com

Furniture, Bedding & Decor .... ✓ ✓ .... Gear & Equipment
Nursing & Feeding .... ✓ ✓ .... Safety & Babycare
Clothing, Shoes & Accessories ...... ✓ ✓ .... Books, Toys & Entertainment

birthandbaby.com ★★★★☆

“*...incredible site for buying a nursing bra... there is more information about different manufacturers than you can imagine... I've even received a phone call from the owner after placing an order to clarify something... free shipping, so it's easy to buy multiple sizes and send back the ones that don't fit... their selection of nursing bras is better than any other place I've found... if you are a hard to fit size, this is the place to go...* ”

Furniture, Bedding & Decor .... ✗ ✓ .... Gear & Equipment
Nursing & Feeding .... ✓ ✓ .... Safety & Babycare
Clothing, Shoes & Accessories ...... ✗ ✓ .... Books, Toys & Entertainment

blueberrybabies.com

Furniture, Bedding & Decor .... ✓ ✓ .... Gear & Equipment
Nursing & Feeding .... ✓ ✓ .... Safety & Babycare
Clothing, Shoes & Accessories ...... ✓ ✓ .... Books, Toys & Entertainment

buybuybaby.com ★★★★½

“*...this is the web site for the popular New York-based baby retailer... you name it, they've got it... all the items in their store can also be found on their web site... prices are fair - especially since things get shipped right to your door... we had some items that were damaged and their online customer service took care of it without any problems...* ”

Furniture, Bedding & Decor .... ✓ ✓ .... Gear & Equipment
Nursing & Feeding .... ✓ ✓ .... Safety & Babycare
Clothing, Shoes & Accessories ...... ✓ ✓ .... Books, Toys & Entertainment

childcarriers.com

Furniture, Bedding & Decor .... ✗ ✓ .... Gear & Equipment

Nursing & Feeding ✗ ✗ Safety & Babycare
Clothing, Shoes & Accessories ✗ ✗ Books, Toys & Entertainment

clothdiaper.com

Furniture, Bedding & Decor ✗ ✓ Gear & Equipment
Nursing & Feeding ✓ ✓ Safety & Babycare
Clothing, Shoes & Accessories ✗ ✗ Books, Toys & Entertainment

cocoacrayon.com

Furniture, Bedding & Decor ✓ ✓ Gear & Equipment
Nursing & Feeding ✓ ✓ Safety & Babycare
Clothing, Shoes & Accessories ✓ ✓ Books, Toys & Entertainment

cvs.com ★★★★☆

"...super convenient web site for any 'drug store' items... items are delivered in a reasonable amount of time... decent selection of baby products... prices are competitive and ordering online definitely beats making the trip out to the drugstore... order a bunch of stuff at a time so shipping is free... I used them for my baby announcements and everyone loved them... super easy to refill prescriptions... it was a real relief to order all my formula, baby wipes and diapers online..."

Furniture, Bedding & Decor ✗ ✗ Gear & Equipment
Nursing & Feeding ✓ ✓ Safety & Babycare
Clothing, Shoes & Accessories ✗ ✗ Books, Toys & Entertainment

dreamtimebaby.com

Furniture, Bedding & Decor ✓ ✓ Gear & Equipment
Nursing & Feeding ✓ ✓ Safety & Babycare
Clothing, Shoes & Accessories ✓ ✓ Books, Toys & Entertainment

drugstore.com ★★★★☆

Furniture, Bedding & Decor ✗ ✗ Gear & Equipment
Nursing & Feeding ✓ ✓ Safety & Babycare
Clothing, Shoes & Accessories ✗ ✗ Books, Toys & Entertainment

ebay.com ★★★★☆

"...great way to save money on everything from maternity clothes to breast pumps... be careful with whom you do business... it's always worth checking out what's available... I picked up a brand new jogger for dirt cheap... great deals to be had if you have patience to browse and be willing to resell or exchange what you don't like... baby stuff is easily found and often reasonably priced... keep an eye on shipping costs when you're bidding..."

Furniture, Bedding & Decor ✓ ✓ Gear & Equipment
Nursing & Feeding ✓ ✓ Safety & Babycare
Clothing, Shoes & Accessories ✓ ✓ Books, Toys & Entertainment

egiggle.com ★★★★☆

"...nice selection—not overwhelming... don't expect the big box store brands here—they carry higher-end, specialty items that you won't find elsewhere... smooth shopping experience... nice site—convenient and easy to use..."

Furniture, Bedding & Decor ✓ ✓ Gear & Equipment
Nursing & Feeding ✓ ✓ Safety & Babycare
Clothing, Shoes & Accessories ✓ ✓ Books, Toys & Entertainment

gagagifts.com ★★★★☆

"...great online store that carries fun clothes and unique gifts and toys for kids and adults... unique and special gifts like designer diaper bags, Whoozit learning toys and handmade quilts... this site makes gift buying incredibly easy—I'm done in less than 5 minutes... prices are high but products are special..."

Furniture, Bedding & Decor .... ✓ ✓ .... Gear & Equipment
Nursing & Feeding .... ✓ ✓ .... Safety & Babycare
Clothing, Shoes & Accessories ...... ✓ ✓ .... Books, Toys & Entertainment

gap.com ★★★★☆

"...I love the Gap's online store—all the cool things in their stores available via my computer... terrific selection of boys and girls clothes plus cute shoes... you can find awesome deals and return online purchases to Gap stores... their clothes are very durable... it's easy to purchase items online and delivery is prompt... a very practical and affordable way to shop... site makes it easy to quickly find what you need... sign up for the weekly newsletter and you'll find out about online sales..."

Furniture, Bedding & Decor .... ✓ ✓ .... Gear & Equipment
Nursing & Feeding .... ✗ ✗ .... Safety & Babycare
Clothing, Shoes & Accessories ...... ✓ ✓ .... Books, Toys & Entertainment

geniusbabies.com ★★★½☆

"...the best selection available of developmental toys and gifts... the only place to order real puppets from the Baby Einstein video series... cool place for unique baby shower and birthday gifts... their site navigation could use an upgrade..."

Furniture, Bedding & Decor .... ✗ ✗ .... Gear & Equipment
Nursing & Feeding .... ✗ ✗ .... Safety & Babycare
Clothing, Shoes & Accessories ...... ✗ ✓ .... Books, Toys & Entertainment

gymboree.com ★★★★☆

"...beautiful clothing and great quality... colorful and stylish baby and kids wear... lots of fun birthday gift ideas... easy exchange and return policy... items usually go on sale pretty quickly... save money with gymbucks... many stores have a play area which makes shopping with my kids fun (let alone feasible)..."

Furniture, Bedding & Decor .... ✗ ✗ .... Gear & Equipment
Nursing & Feeding .... ✗ ✗ .... Safety & Babycare
Clothing, Shoes & Accessories ...... ✓ ✓ .... Books, Toys & Entertainment

hannaandersson.com

Furniture, Bedding & Decor .... ✓ ✗ .... Gear & Equipment
Nursing & Feeding .... ✓ ✗ .... Safety & Babycare
Clothing, Shoes & Accessories ...... ✓ ✓ .... Books, Toys & Entertainment

jcpenney.com

Furniture, Bedding & Decor .... ✓ ✗ .... Gear & Equipment
Nursing & Feeding .... ✗ ✓ .... Safety & Babycare
Clothing, Shoes & Accessories ...... ✓ ✗ .... Books, Toys & Entertainment

joggingstroller.com ★★★★★

"...an excellent resource when you're choosing a jogging stroller... the entire site is devoted to joggers... very helpful information that's worth checking whether you plan to buy from them or not... the best online guide for researching jogging strollers... includes helpful comparisons and parent reviews on the top strollers..."

Furniture, Bedding & Decor .... ✗ ✓ .... Gear & Equipment
Nursing & Feeding .... ✗ ✗ .... Safety & Babycare
Clothing, Shoes & Accessories ...... ✗ ✗ .... Books, Toys & Entertainment

kidsurplus.com

Furniture, Bedding & Decor .... ✓ ✗ .... Gear & Equipment
Nursing & Feeding .... ✓ ✗ .... Safety & Babycare
Clothing, Shoes & Accessories ...... ✓ ✓ .... Books, Toys & Entertainment

landofnod.com

"...cool site with adorable and unique furnishings... hip kid style art work... fabulous furniture and bedding... the catalog is amusing and nicely laid out... lots of sweet selections for both boys and girls... good customer service... fun but small selection of music, books, toys and more... a great way to get ideas for putting rooms together..."

Furniture, Bedding & Decor ✓ | ✗ Gear & Equipment
Nursing & Feeding ✗ | ✗ Safety & Babycare
Clothing, Shoes & Accessories ✗ | ✓ Books, Toys & Entertainment

landsend.com

"...carries the best quality in children's wear—their stuff lasts forever... durable and adorable clothing, shoes and bedding... they offer a huge variety of casual clothing and awesome pajamas... not as inexpensive as other sites, but you can't beat the quality... the very best diaper bags... site is easy to navigate and has great finds for the entire family... love the flannel sheets, maternity clothes and shoes for mom..."

Furniture, Bedding & Decor ✓ | ✗ Gear & Equipment
Nursing & Feeding ✗ | ✗ Safety & Babycare
Clothing, Shoes & Accessories ✓ | ✗ Books, Toys & Entertainment

letsgostrolling.com

Furniture, Bedding & Decor ✓ | ✓ Gear & Equipment
Nursing & Feeding ✓ | ✗ Safety & Babycare
Clothing, Shoes & Accessories ✓ | ✓ Books, Toys & Entertainment

llbean.com

"...high quality clothing for babies, toddlers and kids at reasonable prices... the clothes are extremely durable and stand up to wear and tear very well... a great site for winter clothing and gear shopping... wonderful selection for older kids, too... fewer options for infants... an awesome way to shop for clothing basics... you can't beat the diaper bags..."

Furniture, Bedding & Decor ✗ | ✗ Gear & Equipment
Nursing & Feeding ✗ | ✗ Safety & Babycare
Clothing, Shoes & Accessories ✓ | ✗ Books, Toys & Entertainment

modernseed.com

"...it was fun finding many unique items for my son's nursery... I wanted a contemporary theme and they had lots of wonderful items including crib linens, wall art and lighting... the place to find super cool baby and kid stuff and the best place for modern nursery decor... they also carry children and adult clothing and furniture and toys... not cheap but one of my favorite places..."

Furniture, Bedding & Decor ✓ | ✓ Gear & Equipment
Nursing & Feeding ✓ | ✓ Safety & Babycare
Clothing, Shoes & Accessories ✓ | ✓ Books, Toys & Entertainment

naturalbaby-catalog.com

"...all natural products—clothes, toys, herbal medicines, bathing, etc... fine quality and a great alternative to the usual products... site is fairly easy to navigate and has a good selection... dealing with returns is pretty painless... love the catalogue and the products... excellent customer service... lots of organic clothing made with natural materials... high quality shoes in a range of prices..."

Furniture, Bedding & Decor ✓ | ✓ Gear & Equipment
Nursing & Feeding ✓ | ✓ Safety & Babycare
Clothing, Shoes & Accessories ✓ | ✓ Books, Toys & Entertainment

netkidswear.com

Furniture, Bedding & Decor	✓	✓	Gear & Equipment
Nursing & Feeding	✓	✓	Safety & Babycare
Clothing, Shoes & Accessories	✓	✓	Books, Toys & Entertainment

nordstrom.com ★★★★☆

"...just like their stores, the site carries a great selection of high-quality items... you can't go wrong with Nordstrom—even online... quick shipping and easy site navigation... a little pricey, but great quality items... I've purchased a bunch of baby stuff from their website and have never had a problem... a great shoe selection for all ages..."

Furniture, Bedding & Decor	✓	✓	Gear & Equipment
Nursing & Feeding	✗	✓	Safety & Babycare
Clothing, Shoes & Accessories	✓	✓	Books, Toys & Entertainment

oldnavy.com ★★★★☆

"...shopping online with Old Navy makes it easy to find incredible bargains... site was easy to use and my products arrived quickly... site carries items that aren't necessarily available in their stores... an inexpensive way to get trendy baby clothes... you can return items directly to any store... check out the sale page of this web site for deep discounts on current season clothing... I signed up for the email savings and get free shipping several times a year..."

Furniture, Bedding & Decor	✗	✗	Gear & Equipment
Nursing & Feeding	✗	✗	Safety & Babycare
Clothing, Shoes & Accessories	✓	✗	Books, Toys & Entertainment

oliebollen.com ★★★★½

"...perfect for the busy mom looking for a fun baby shower gift... this online-only store has all the best brands—Catamini and Tea Collection to name a couple... great for gifts and home stuff, too... lots of style... very easy to use... 30 days full refund, 60 days store credit..."

Furniture, Bedding & Decor	✓	✗	Gear & Equipment
Nursing & Feeding	✓	✗	Safety & Babycare
Clothing, Shoes & Accessories	✓	✓	Books, Toys & Entertainment

onestepahead.com ★★★★½

"...one stop shopping site with everything parents are looking for... huge variety of items to choose from... I bought everything from a crib to a nursery bottle... high quality items, many of which are developmental in nature... great line of safety equipment... easy to order and fast delivery but you will pay for shipping... web site has helpful reviews... great site for hard to find items..."

Furniture, Bedding & Decor	✓	✓	Gear & Equipment
Nursing & Feeding	✓	✓	Safety & Babycare
Clothing, Shoes & Accessories	✓	✓	Books, Toys & Entertainment

peapods.com

Furniture, Bedding & Decor	✓	✓	Gear & Equipment
Nursing & Feeding	✗	✓	Safety & Babycare
Clothing, Shoes & Accessories	✓	✓	Books, Toys & Entertainment

pokkadots.com

Furniture, Bedding & Decor	✓	✓	Gear & Equipment
Nursing & Feeding	✓	✗	Safety & Babycare
Clothing, Shoes & Accessories	✓	✓	Books, Toys & Entertainment

poshtots.com ★★★★☆

"...incredible selection of whimsical and out-of-the-ordinary nursery decor... beautiful, unique designer room sets in multiple styles... they do boys and girls bedrooms... great for the baby that has everything—

including parents with an unlimited cash account... you can get great ideas about decor just from browsing the site, even if you don't buy... **"**

Furniture, Bedding & Decor ✓ — ✓ Gear & Equipment
Nursing & Feeding ✓ — ✗ Safety & Babycare
Clothing, Shoes & Accessories ✓ — ✓ Books, Toys & Entertainment

potterybarnkids.com ★★★★½

"*...beautiful high end furniture and bedding... they have a way with matching everything perfectly and I am always a sucker for that look... adorable merchandise of great quality... you will get what you pay for: high quality furniture at high prices... web site is easy to navigate... items like hooded towels and plush blankets make this place special... if I could afford it I would buy everything in the store...* **"**

Furniture, Bedding & Decor ✓ — ✓ Gear & Equipment
Nursing & Feeding ✗ — ✗ Safety & Babycare
Clothing, Shoes & Accessories ✗ — ✓ Books, Toys & Entertainment

preemie.com

Furniture, Bedding & Decor ✗ — ✓ Gear & Equipment
Nursing & Feeding ✓ — ✓ Safety & Babycare
Clothing, Shoes & Accessories ✓ — ✓ Books, Toys & Entertainment

rei.com

Furniture, Bedding & Decor ✗ — ✓ Gear & Equipment
Nursing & Feeding ✗ — ✗ Safety & Babycare
Clothing, Shoes & Accessories ✓ — ✓ Books, Toys & Entertainment

royalnursery.com ★★★½☆

"*...this used to be a store in San Diego and now it is only online... if you need a silver rattle, luxury baby blanket or shower gift—this is the place... a beautiful site with elegant baby clothes, jewelry, and gifts...love the hand print kits—they are my current favorite gift... high end baby wear and gear... be sure to check out the sale items...* **"**

Furniture, Bedding & Decor ✓ — ✗ Gear & Equipment
Nursing & Feeding ✗ — ✓ Safety & Babycare
Clothing, Shoes & Accessories ✓ — ✓ Books, Toys & Entertainment

showeryourbaby.com

Furniture, Bedding & Decor ✓ — ✓ Gear & Equipment
Nursing & Feeding ✓ — ✓ Safety & Babycare
Clothing, Shoes & Accessories ✓ — ✓ Books, Toys & Entertainment

snipsnsnails.com ★★★★☆

"*...a great boys clothing store for infants to 14 years old... clothes for every occasion, from casual to special occasion... pajamas and swimsuits, too... pricey, but upscale and fun... items on the web site are not always in stock ...* **"**

Furniture, Bedding & Decor ✓ — ✗ Gear & Equipment
Nursing & Feeding ✗ — ✗ Safety & Babycare
Clothing, Shoes & Accessories ✓ — ✗ Books, Toys & Entertainment

strollerdepot.com

Furniture, Bedding & Decor ✗ — ✓ Gear & Equipment
Nursing & Feeding ✗ — ✗ Safety & Babycare
Clothing, Shoes & Accessories ✗ — ✓ Books, Toys & Entertainment

strollers4less.com ★★★½☆

"*...some of the best prices on strollers... I love this site... we purchased our stroller online for a lot less than it costs locally... online ordering went smoothly—from ordering through receiving... wide* selection and some incredible deals... shipping is relatively fast... free shipping if you spend $100, which isn't hard to do... ”

Furniture, Bedding & Decor ✗ ✓ Gear & Equipment
Nursing & Feeding ✗ ✗ Safety & Babycare
Clothing, Shoes & Accessories ✗ ✓ Books, Toys & Entertainment

target.com ★★★★☆

“...our favorite place to shop for kids stuff—good selection and very affordable... guilt free shopping—kids grow so fast so I don't want to pay high department store prices... everything from diapers and sippy cups to car seats and strollers... easy return policy... decent registry that won't freak your friends out with outrageous prices... easy, convenient shopping for well-priced items... all the big box brands available—Graco, Evenflo, Eddie Bauer, etc.... ”

Furniture, Bedding & Decor ✓ ✓ Gear & Equipment
Nursing & Feeding ✓ ✓ Safety & Babycare
Clothing, Shoes & Accessories ✓ ✓ Books, Toys & Entertainment

teddylux.com

Furniture, Bedding & Decor ✗ ✗ Gear & Equipment
Nursing & Feeding ✗ ✗ Safety & Babycare
Clothing, Shoes & Accessories ✗ ✓ Books, Toys & Entertainment

thebabyhammock.com ★★★★☆

“...a family owned business selling parent-tested products from morning sickness relief products to baby carriers, natural skincare, gift sets and more... fast friendly service... natural products and waldorf influenced toys... ”

Furniture, Bedding & Decor ✓ ✓ Gear & Equipment
Nursing & Feeding ✓ ✓ Safety & Babycare
Clothing, Shoes & Accessories ✓ ✗ Books, Toys & Entertainment

thebabyoutlet.com

Furniture, Bedding & Decor ✗ ✓ Gear & Equipment
Nursing & Feeding ✓ ✓ Safety & Babycare
Clothing, Shoes & Accessories ✗ ✓ Books, Toys & Entertainment

tinyride.com

Furniture, Bedding & Decor ✗ ✓ Gear & Equipment
Nursing & Feeding ✓ ✗ Safety & Babycare
Clothing, Shoes & Accessories ✗ ✗ Books, Toys & Entertainment

toadsandtulips.com

Furniture, Bedding & Decor ✓ ✗ Gear & Equipment
Nursing & Feeding ✗ ✗ Safety & Babycare
Clothing, Shoes & Accessories ✓ ✓ Books, Toys & Entertainment

toysrus.com ★★★★☆

“...makes shopping incredibly easy... well organized site with discount prices... makes registering for gifts super simple... even more products are online than in the actual stores... check out the outlet section and coupon codes for even more discounts... I did most of my Christmas shopping here, paid no shipping and had my gifts delivered in 3 days... web site includes helpful toy reviews... use this to send your wish lists to relatives... ”

Furniture, Bedding & Decor ✓ ✓ Gear & Equipment
Nursing & Feeding ✓ ✓ Safety & Babycare
Clothing, Shoes & Accessories ✓ ✓ Books, Toys & Entertainment

tuttibella.com ★★★★☆

“...well designed web site with beautiful, original clothing, toys, bedding and accessories... cute vintage stuff for babies and kids...

stylish designer goods from here and abroad... your child will stand out among the Baby Gap-clothed masses... gorgeous fabrics... a great place to find that perfect gift for someone special and stylish... ”

Furniture, Bedding & Decor .... ✓ ✓ .... Gear & Equipment
Nursing & Feeding .... ✗ ✗ .... Safety & Babycare
Clothing, Shoes & Accessories .... ✓ ✗ .... Books, Toys & Entertainment

usillygoose.com

Furniture, Bedding & Decor .... ✓ ✗ .... Gear & Equipment
Nursing & Feeding .... ✗ ✗ .... Safety & Babycare
Clothing, Shoes & Accessories .... ✗ ✓ .... Books, Toys & Entertainment

walmart.com ★★★½☆

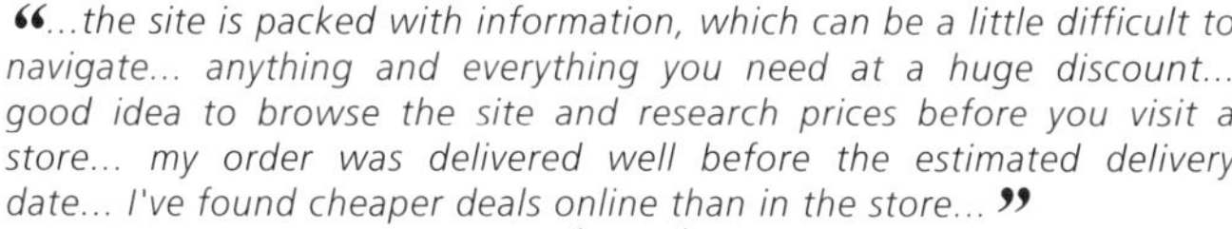

“*...the site is packed with information, which can be a little difficult to navigate... anything and everything you need at a huge discount... good idea to browse the site and research prices before you visit a store... my order was delivered well before the estimated delivery date... I've found cheaper deals online than in the store...* ”

Furniture, Bedding & Decor .... ✓ ✓ .... Gear & Equipment
Nursing & Feeding .... ✓ ✓ .... Safety & Babycare
Clothing, Shoes & Accessories .... ✓ ✓ .... Books, Toys & Entertainment

maternity clothing

Baltimore City

"lila picks"

★Tummies Maternity

Baby Depot

"...a surprisingly good selection of maternity clothes at great prices... staff can be hard to find so be prepared to dig... cute pants, skirts and sets... I wouldn't have thought that their selection would be as good as it is... not much other than casual items, but what they have is pretty good..."

Casual wear .... ✓ $$ .... Prices
Business wear .... × ❸ .... Product availability
Intimate apparel .... × ❸ .... Customer service
Nursing wear .... × ❸ .... Decor

WWW.BABYDEPOT.COM

BALTIMORE—1955 E JOPPA RD (AT PERRING PKWY); 410.665.1390; M-SA 10-9:30, SU 11-6

BALTIMORE—6500 REISTERSTOWN RD (AT REISTERTOWN MALL); 410.764.3338; M-SA 10-9, SU 12-6; PARKING LOT AT MALL

BALTIMORE—6901 SECURITY BLVD (AT BELMONT AVE); 410.265.1508; M-SA 10-9:30, SU 11-6; LOT

H & M

"...hip, cute and cheap maternity clothes... wonderful stretch pants without the cutout for tummy... great style... lots of cool clothes, but need to visit often, as selection changes frequently... you can find some hip business type clothes on sale... not the place to go for personalized service..."

Casual wear .... ✓ $$ .... Prices
Business wear .... ✓ ❸ .... Product availability
Intimate apparel .... ✓ ❸ .... Customer service
Nursing wear .... × ❸ .... Decor

WWW.HM.COM

BALTIMORE—8200 PERRY HALL BLVD (AT HONEYGO BLVD); 410.931.9373; M-SA 10-9, SU 11-6

JCPenney

"...competitive prices and a surprisingly cute selection... they carry bigger sizes that are very hard to find at other stores... much cheaper than most maternity boutiques and they always seem to have some sort of sale going on... an especially large selection of maternity jeans for plus sizes... a more conservative collection than the smaller, hipper boutiques... good for casual basics, but not much for special occasions..."

Casual wear .... ✓ $$ .... Prices
Business wear .... ✓ ❸ .... Product availability
Intimate apparel .... ✓ ❸ .... Customer service
Nursing wear .... × ❸ .... Decor

WWW.JCPENNEY.COM

BALTIMORE—7777 EASTPOINT MALL (AT EASTPOINT MALL); 410.288.5800; M-F 9:30-9:30, SA 9-9:30, SU 11-6; LOT

Old Navy

"...the best for casual maternity clothing like stretchy T-shirts with Lycra and comfy jeans... prices are so reasonable it's ridiculous... not much for the workplace, but you can't beat the prices on casual ware... not all Old Navy locations carry their maternity line... don't expect a huge or diverse selection... the staff is not always knowledgeable about maternity clothing and can't really help with questions about sizing... they have the best return policy—order online and return to the nearest store location... perfect for inexpensive maternity duds..."

Casual wear ✓ | $$ Prices
Business wear ✗ | ❹ Product availability
Intimate apparel ✗ | ❸ Customer service
Nursing wear ✗ | ❸ Decor

WWW.OLDNAVY.COM

BALTIMORE—6901 SECURITY SQ BLVD (AT SECURITY SQ MALL); 443.436.5808; M-SA 10-9:30, SU 12-6

Raw Sugar

"...I love shopping here—the atmosphere is welcoming and the selection is outstanding... not as much as some of the other chain stores, but they carry things you won't find elsewhere... higher-end clothing for moms and kids... locally owned... wonderful atmosphere..."

Casual wear ✓ | $$$ Prices
Business wear ✗ | ❸ Product availability
Intimate apparel ✗ | ❸ Customer service
Nursing wear ✗ | ❸ Decor

WWW.RAWSUGARONLINE.COM

BALTIMORE—524 BELVEDERE AVE (AT YORK RD); 410.464.1240; M-SA 10-6, SU 11-5; STREET PARKING

Sears

"...good place to get maternity clothes for a low price... the clearance rack always has good deals and their sales are quite frequent... not necessarily super high quality but if you just need them for 9 months, who cares... good selection of nursing bras... I love the fact that they carry maternity wear in larger sizes—I got so tired of looking in those cutesy boutiques and then being disappointed because they didn't have my size... the only place I found maternity for plus-sized women..."

Casual wear ✓ | $$ Prices
Business wear ✗ | ❸ Product availability
Intimate apparel ✓ | ❸ Customer service
Nursing wear ✓ | ❸ Decor

WWW.SEARS.COM

BALTIMORE—6901 SECURITY BLVD (AT SECURITY SQ MALL OFF I-695); 410.281.2255; M-SA 10-9:30, SU 11-6; LOT

BALTIMORE—7885 EASTERN AVE (AT NORTH POINT BLVD); 410.288.7700; M-F 10-9, SA 8-6, SU 11-5; LOT

BALTIMORE—8200 PERRY HALL BLVD (AT HONEYGO BLVD); 410.931.5555; M-F 10-9, SA 10-6, SU 11-5; LOT

Target

"...I was surprised at how fashionable their selection is—they carry Liz Lange and other really cute selections... the price is right—especially since you'll only be wearing these clothes for a few months... great for maternity basics—T-shirts, skirts, sweaters, even maternity bras... best of all, you can do some maternity shopping while you're shopping for

maternity

other household basics... shirts for $10—you can't beat that... not the most exciting or romantic maternity shopping, but once you see the prices you'll get over it... as always, Target provides the perfectly priced solution... ”

Casual wear	✓	$$	Prices
Business wear	✓	❸	Product availability
Intimate apparel	✓	❸	Customer service
Nursing wear	✓	❸	Decor

WWW.TARGET.COM

BALTIMORE—5230 CAMPBELL BLVD (AT I 95); 410.933.9632; M-SA 8-10, SU 8-9; LOT

Tummies Maternity

“*...wonderful styles—cute and flattering for my bulging belly... the staff is knowledgeable and helpful—I was tired of getting zero service at the chains... their prices are a little higher, but I enjoy shopping here so I don't mind paying a little extra... awesome selection of career wear... a must-see for all new Baltimore moms...* ”

Casual wear	✓	$$$	Prices
Business wear	✓	❸	Product availability
Intimate apparel	✓	❸	Customer service
Nursing wear	✓	❸	Decor

WWW.TUMMIESMATERNITY.COM

BALTIMORE—25 HOOKS LN (OFF REISTERSTOWN RD); 410.602.5388; M T TH 10-5, W 12-8, F 10-4, SU 11-3

North of Baltimore

★Maternity Wardrobe

Baby Depot

"...a surprisingly good selection of maternity clothes at great prices... staff can be hard to find so be prepared to dig... cute pants, skirts and sets... I wouldn't have thought that their selection would be as good as it is... not much other than casual items, but what they have is pretty good..."

Casual wear	✓	$$	Prices
Business wear	✗	❸	Product availability
Intimate apparel	✗	❸	Customer service
Nursing wear	✗	❸	Decor

WWW.BABYDEPOT.COM

HUNT VALLEY—118 SHAWAN RD (AT HUNT VALLEY MALL); 410.584.7407; M-SA 10-9:30, SU 11-6

Kohl's

"...a small maternity selection but I always manage to find several items I like... our favorite shopping destination—clean, wide open aisles... not a huge amount of maternity, but if you find something the price is always right... the selection is very inconsistent but sometimes you can find nice casuals... best for the bare bone basics like T-shirts, shorts or casual pants..."

Casual wear	✓	$$	Prices
Business wear	✗	❸	Product availability
Intimate apparel	✗	❸	Customer service
Nursing wear	✗	❸	Decor

WWW.KOHLS.COM

BEL AIR—5 BEL AIR SOUTH PKWY (AT EMMORTON RD); 410.569.6066; M-SA 8-10, SU 10-8

Maternity Wardrobe

"...best in town and you will not look like everyone else... worth the trip—amazing selection of designers... knowledgeable staff... good store to find some brand name maternity clothes... good to get away from the usual clothes available at the bigger chain stores... they carry some nice items that I couldn't find anywhere else..."

Casual wear	✓	$$$$	Prices
Business wear	✓	❹	Product availability
Intimate apparel	✓	❺	Customer service
Nursing wear	✓	❹	Decor

HUNT VALLEY—118 SHAWAN RD (AT HUNT VALLEY CTR); 410.527.3480; M-SA 10-8, SU 12-5

Mimi Maternity

"...it's definitely worth stopping here if you're still working and need some good looking outfits... not cheap, but the quality is fantastic... not as expensive as A Pea In The Pod, but better quality than Motherhood Maternity... nice for basics that will last you through multiple pregnancies... perfect for work clothes, but pricey for the everyday stuff... good deals to be found on their sales racks... a good mix of high-end fancy clothes and items you can wear every day..."

Casual wear	✓	$$$	Prices
Business wear	✓	❹	Product availability
Intimate apparel	✓	❹	Customer service
Nursing wear	✓	❹	Decor

WWW.MIMIMATERNITY.COM

TOWSON—825 DULANEY VALLEY RD (AT TOWSON TOWN CTR); 410.296.1245; M-SA 10-9:30, SU 11-6

Old Navy

"...the best for casual maternity clothing like stretchy T-shirts with Lycra and comfy jeans... prices are so reasonable it's ridiculous... not much for the workplace, but you can't beat the prices on casual ware... not all Old Navy locations carry their maternity line... don't expect a huge or diverse selection... the staff is not always knowledgeable about maternity clothing and can't really help with questions about sizing... they have the best return policy—order online and return to the nearest store location... perfect for inexpensive maternity duds..."

Casual wear	✓	$$	Prices
Business wear	✗	❹	Product availability
Intimate apparel	✗	❸	Customer service
Nursing wear	✗	❸	Decor

WWW.OLDNAVY.COM

BEL AIR—678 BEL AIR RD (AT HARFORD MALL); 410.638.6780; M-SA 10-9:30, SU 11-5; LOT

Ross Dress For Less

"...if you don't mind looking through a lot of clothes you can find some good pieces at great prices... they sometimes have larger sizes too... totally hit or miss depending on their most recent shipment... not the most fashionable clothing, but great for that everyday, casual T shirt or stretchy pair of pants..."

Casual wear	✓	$$$	Prices
Business wear	✗	❸	Product availability
Intimate apparel	✗	❷	Customer service
Nursing wear	✗	❷	Decor

WWW.ROSSSTORES.COM

PARKVILLE—8888 WALTHAM WOODS RD (AT PERRING PKWY); 410.661.7390; M-SA 9:30-9:30, SU 11-7; LOT

Sears

"...good place to get maternity clothes for a low price... the clearance rack always has good deals and their sales are quite frequent... not necessarily super high quality but if you just need them for 9 months, who cares... good selection of nursing bras... I love the fact that they carry maternity wear in larger sizes—I got so tired of looking in those cutesy boutiques and then being disappointed because they didn't have my size... the only place I found maternity for plus-sized women..."

Casual wear	✓	$$	Prices
Business wear	✗	❸	Product availability
Intimate apparel	✓	❸	Customer service
Nursing wear	✓	❸	Decor

WWW.SEARS.COM

BEL AIR—658 BALTIMORE PIKE (AT HARFORD MALL); 410.588.5000; M-F 9:30-9:30, SA 9-10, SU 10-6; LOT

COCKEYSVILLE—126 SHAWAN RD (AT YORK RD); 410.771.8355; M-F 9:30-9:30, SA 8-9:30, SU 10-6; LOT

Target

"...I was surprised at how fashionable their selection is—they carry Liz Lange and other really cute selections... the price is right—especially since you'll only be wearing these clothes for a few months... great for maternity basics—T-shirts, skirts, sweaters, even maternity bras... best of all, you can do some maternity shopping while you're shopping for other household basics... shirts for $10—you can't beat that... not the most exciting or romantic maternity shopping, but once you see the prices you'll get over it... as always, Target provides the perfectly priced solution..."

Casual wear ✓ | $$ Prices
Business wear ✓ | ❸ Product availability
Intimate apparel ✓ | ❸ Customer service
Nursing wear ✓ | ❸ Decor

WWW.TARGET.COM

BEL AIR—580 MARKETPLACE DR (AT HWY 24); 410.638.7532; M-SA 8-10, SU 8-9

TOWSON—1238 PUTTY HILL AVE (AT TOWSON PL); 410.823.4423; M-SA 8-10, SU 8-9; LOT

Tried But True

"...a nice selection of maternity and children's clothing... I hate spending so much money on clothes I know I'm only going to be wearing for a short time—it's nice to be able to come here and pick up just a few items without spending a lot... the staff is friendly and helpful..."

Casual wear ✓ | $$ Prices
Business wear ✓ | ❺ Product availability
Intimate apparel ✗ | ❺ Customer service
Nursing wear ✗ | ❹ Decor

COCKEYSVILLE—10744 YORK RD (AT ROBERTS RD); 410.666.9265; M W F-SA 10-4, T TH 10-5, SU 12-5; LOT

maternity

West of Baltimore

"lila picks"

★Motherhood Maternity

H & M

"...hip, cute and cheap maternity clothes... wonderful stretch pants without the cutout for tummy... great style... lots of cool clothes, but need to visit often, as selection changes frequently... you can find some hip business type clothes on sale... not the place to go for personalized service..."

Casual wear ✓ | $$ Prices
Business wear ✓ | ❸ Product availability
Intimate apparel ✓ | ❸ Customer service
Nursing wear ✗ | ❸ Dccor

WWW.HM.COM

OWINGS MILLS—10300 MILL RUN CIR (AT OWINGS MILLS TOWN CTR); 443.394.0291; M-SA 10-9, SU 11-6

JCPenney

"...competitive prices and a surprisingly cute selection... they carry bigger sizes that are very hard to find at other stores... much cheaper than most maternity boutiques and they always seem to have some sort of sale going on... an especially large selection of maternity jeans for plus sizes... a more conservative collection than the smaller, hipper boutiques... good for casual basics, but not much for special occasions..."

Casual wear ✓ | $$ Prices
Business wear ✓ | ❸ Product availability
Intimate apparel ✓ | ❸ Customer service
Nursing wear ✗ | ❸ Decor

WWW.JCPENNEY.COM

OWINGS MILLS—10400 MILL RUN CIR (AT OWINGS MILLS BLVD); 410.902.9400; M-SA 10-9:30, SU 11-7; LOT

Macy's

"...if your local Macy's has a maternity section, you're in luck—call ahead!.. I bought my entire pregnancy work wardrobe at Macy's... the styles are all relatively recent and the brands are well known... you can generally find some attractive dresses at very reasonable prices on their sales rack... like other large department stores, you're bound to find something that works if you dig enough... very convenient because you can get your other shopping done at the same time... the selection isn't huge, but what they have is nice..."

Casual wear ✓ | $$$ Prices
Business wear ✓ | ❸ Product availability
Intimate apparel ✓ | ❸ Customer service
Nursing wear ✗ | ❸ Decor

WWW.MACYS.COM

OWINGS MILLS—10200 MILL RUN CIR (AT OWING MILLS TOWN CTR); 410.363.7400; M-TH 10-9:30, F-SA 10-10, SU 11-6

Motherhood Maternity

"...a wide variety of styles, from business to weekend wear—all at a good price... affordable and cute... everything from bras and swimsuits to work outfits... highly recommended for those who don't want to spend a fortune on maternity clothes... less fancy and pricey than their sister stores—A Pea in the Pod and Mimi Maternity... they have frequent sales, so you just need to keep dropping in—you're bound to find something good..."

Casual wear ✓ | $$$ Prices
Business wear ✓ | ❹ Product availability
Intimate apparel ✓ | ❹ Customer service
Nursing wear ✓ | ❸ Decor

WWW.MOTHERHOOD.COM

OWINGS MILLS—10300 MILL RUN CIR (AT OWINGS MILLS TOWN CTR); 410.654.1468; M-SA 10-9:30, SU 11-6

Ross Dress For Less

"...if you don't mind looking through a lot of clothes you can find some good pieces at great prices... they sometimes have larger sizes too... totally hit or miss depending on their most recent shipment... not the most fashionable clothing, but great for that everyday, casual T shirt or stretchy pair of pants..."

Casual wear ✓ | $$$ Prices
Business wear ✗ | ❸ Product availability
Intimate apparel ✗ | ❷ Customer service
Nursing wear ✗ | ❷ Decor

WWW.ROSSSTORES.COM

OWINGS MILLS—9616 REISTERSTOWN RD (AT VALLEY CTR); 410.363.8001; M-SA 9:30-9:30, SU 11-7; LOT

Target

"...I was surprised at how fashionable their selection is—they carry Liz Lange and other really cute selections... the price is right—especially since you'll only be wearing these clothes for a few months... great for maternity basics—T-shirts, skirts, sweaters, even maternity bras... best of all, you can do some maternity shopping while you're shopping for other household basics... shirts for $10—you can't beat that... not the most exciting or romantic maternity shopping, but once you see the prices you'll get over it... as always, Target provides the perfectly priced solution..."

Casual wear ✓ | $$ Prices
Business wear ✓ | ❸ Product availability
Intimate apparel ✓ | ❸ Customer service
Nursing wear ✓ | ❸ Decor

WWW.TARGET.COM

OWINGS MILLS—11200 REISTERSTOWN RD (AT OWINGS MILLS BLVD); 410.654.9800; M-SA 8-10, SU 8-9; LOT

PIKESVILLE—1737 REISTERSTOWN RD (AT I 695); 410.486.4141; M-SA 8-10, SU 8-9; LOT

South of Baltimore

"lila picks"

★Big Chicks Little Chicks

Baby Depot

"...a surprisingly good selection of maternity clothes at great prices... staff can be hard to find so be prepared to dig... cute pants, skirts and sets... I wouldn't have thought that their selection would be as good as it is... not much other than casual items, but what they have is pretty good..."

Casual wear	✓	$$	Prices
Business wear	✗	❸	Product availability
Intimate apparel	✗	❸	Customer service
Nursing wear	✗	❸	Decor

WWW.BABYDEPOT.COM

ANNAPOLIS—2639 HOUSLEY RD (AT HIGHWAY 450); 410.571.6818; M-SA 10-9, SU 11-6; LOT

HANOVER—7000 ARUNDEL MILLS CIR (AT ARUNDEL MILLS MALL); 410.799.7450; M-SA 10-9:30, SU 11-7

Big Chicks Little Chicks

"...my favorite maternity store ever—they carry unique and trendy maternity clothes that make you feel stylish despite having a belly... owners and staff extremely helpful and knowledgeable... prices are fair and the shopping experience is great..."

Casual wear	✓	$$$$$	Prices
Business wear	✓	❺	Product availability
Intimate apparel	✗	❺	Customer service
Nursing wear	✗	❺	Decor

WWW.BIGCHICKSLITTLECHICKS.COM

EDGEWATER—153 MITCHELLS CHANCE RD (AT STEPNEY LN); 410.956.0684; T-TH 10-7, F-SA 10-6, SU 12-4; FREE PARKING

Fashion Bug

"...not the hippest collection around, but the clothes are really cheap and perfectly presentable... basics like cropped pants and babydoll shirts... plus-sizes are a 'plus' in my book... sale prices are great... check the web for coupons..."

Casual wear	✓	$$$	Prices
Business wear	✓	❸	Product availability
Intimate apparel	✓	❸	Customer service
Nursing wear	✓	❹	Decor

WWW.FASHIONBUG.COM

ARBUTUS—1052 MAIDEN CHOICE LN (AT WESTLAND BLVD), 410.247.0170; M-TH 10-8, F-SA 10-9, SU 12-5

GLEN BURNIE—7385 BALT ANNAPOLIS BLVD (AT 8TH AVE); 410.760.0371; M-SA 10-9, SU 12-6; FREE PARKING

GLEN BURNIE—7990 CRAIN HWY (OFF RT 97); 410.969.2543; M-SA 10-9, SU 12-6; FREE PARKING

H & M

“...hip, cute and cheap maternity clothes... wonderful stretch pants without the cutout for tummy... great style... lots of cool clothes, but need to visit often, as selection changes frequently... you can find some hip business type clothes on sale... not the place to go for personalized service...”

Casual wear ✓ | $$ Prices
Business wear ✓ | ❸ Product availability
Intimate apparel ✓ | ❸ Customer service
Nursing wear ✗ | ❸ Decor

WWW.HM.COM

HANOVER—7000 ARUNDEL MILLS CIR (AT ARUNDEL MILLS CTR); 410.799.0824; M-SA 10-9:30, SU 11-7; STREET AND LOT

JCPenney

“...competitive prices and a surprisingly cute selection... they carry bigger sizes that are very hard to find at other stores... much cheaper than most maternity boutiques and they always seem to have some sort of sale going on... an especially large selection of maternity jeans for plus sizes... a more conservative collection than the smaller, hipper boutiques... good for casual basics, but not much for special occasions...”

Casual wear ✓ | $$ Prices
Business wear ✓ | ❸ Product availability
Intimate apparel ✓ | ❸ Customer service
Nursing wear ✗ | ❸ Decor

WWW.JCPENNEY.COM

ANNAPOLIS—1695 ANNAPOLIS MALL (AT ANNAPOLIS MALL); 410.224.6500; M-SA 10-9:30, SU 11-6; LOT

GLEN BURNIE—7900 RITCHIE HWY (AT MARLEY STATION SHOPPING CTR); 410.760.7724; M-SA 10-9:30, SU 11-6; LOT

Kohl's

“...a small maternity selection but I always manage to find several items I like... our favorite shopping destination—clean, wide open aisles... not a huge amount of maternity, but if you find something the price is always right... the selection is very inconsistent but sometimes you can find nice casuals... best for the bare bone basics like T-shirts, shorts or casual pants...”

Casual wear ✓ | $$ Prices
Business wear ✗ | ❸ Product availability
Intimate apparel ✗ | ❸ Customer service
Nursing wear ✗ | ❸ Decor

WWW.KOHLS.COM

SEVERNA PARK—575 RITCHIE HWY (AT ROBINSON RD); 410.544.6993; M-SA 8-10, SU 10-8

Macy's

“...if your local Macy's has a maternity section, you're in luck—call ahead!.. I bought my entire pregnancy work wardrobe at Macy's... the styles are all relatively recent and the brands are well known... you can generally find some attractive dresses at very reasonable prices on their sales rack... like other large department stores, you're bound to find something that works if you dig enough... very convenient because you can get your other shopping done at the same time... the selection isn't huge, but what they have is nice...”

Casual wear ✓ | $$$ Prices
Business wear ✓ | ❸ Product availability

Intimate apparel .... ✓ ❸ .... Customer service
Nursing wear .... ✗ ❸ .... Decor

WWW.MACYS.COM

GLEN BURNIE—7900 RITCHIE HWY (AT MARLEY STATION SHOPPING CTR); 410.760.2100; M-F 10-9, SA 10-9:30, SU 11-6; LOT

Motherhood Maternity ★★★★☆

"...a wide variety of styles, from business to weekend wear—all at a good price... affordable and cute... everything from bras and swimsuits to work outfits... highly recommended for those who don't want to spend a fortune on maternity clothes... less fancy and pricey than their sister stores—A Pea in the Pod and Mimi Maternity... they have frequent sales, so you just need to keep dropping in—you're bound to find something good..."

Casual wear .... ✓ $$$ .... Prices
Business wear .... ✓ ❹ .... Product availability
Intimate apparel .... ✓ ❹ .... Customer service
Nursing wear .... ✓ ❸ .... Decor

WWW.MOTHERHOOD.COM

ANNAPOLIS—1450 ANNAPOLIS MALL (AT ANNAPOLIS MALL); 410.266.5258; M-SA 10-9:30, SU 11-6; PARKING LOT AT MALL

GLEN BURNIE—7880 RITCHIE HWY (AT MARLEY STATION SHOPPING CTR); 410.768.0883; M-SA 10-9:30, SU 11-6

HANOVER—700 ARUNDEL MILLS CIR (AT ARUNDEL MILLS MALL); 443.755.1770; M-SA 10-9:30, SU 11-7; PARKING LOT AT MALL

Old Navy ★★★½☆

"...the best for casual maternity clothing like stretchy T-shirts with Lycra and comfy jeans... prices are so reasonable it's ridiculous... not much for the workplace, but you can't beat the prices on casual ware... not all Old Navy locations carry their maternity line... don't expect a huge or diverse selection... the staff is not always knowledgeable about maternity clothing and can't really help with questions about sizing... they have the best return policy—order online and return to the nearest store location... perfect for inexpensive maternity duds..."

Casual wear .... ✓ $$ .... Prices
Business wear .... ✗ ❹ .... Product availability
Intimate apparel .... ✗ ❸ .... Customer service
Nursing wear .... ✗ ❸ .... Decor

WWW.OLDNAVY.COM

ANNAPOLIS—2532 SOLOMONS ISLAND RD (AT ARIS T ALLEN BLVD); 410.573.9110; M-SA 9-9, SU 10-6; LOT

HANOVER—7000 ARUNDEL MILLS CIR (AT ARUNDEL MILLS MALL); 443.755.0416; M-SA 10-9:30, SU 11-7; PARKING LOT AT MALL

SEVERNA PARK—571 RITCHIE HWY (AT MCKINSEY RD); 410.384.9267; M-SA 9-9, SU 11-6; LOT

Sears ★★★☆☆

"...good place to get maternity clothes for a low price... the clearance rack always has good deals and their sales are quite frequent... not necessarily super high quality but if you just need them for 9 months, who cares... good selection of nursing bras... I love the fact that they carry maternity wear in larger sizes—I got so tired of looking in those cutesy boutiques and then being disappointed because they didn't have my size... the only place I found maternity for plus-sized women..."

Casual wear .... ✓ $$ .... Prices
Business wear .... ✗ ❸ .... Product availability
Intimate apparel .... ✓ ❸ .... Customer service
Nursing wear .... ✓ ❸ .... Decor

WWW.SEARS.COM

ANNAPOLIS—1040 ANNAPOLIS MALL (AT JENNIFER RD); 443.926.5200; M-F10-9, SA 10-6, SU 11-5; LOT

GLEN BURNIE—7900 GOV RITCHIE HWY (AT MARLEY STATION RD); 410.590.2400; M-F 9:30-9:30, SA 8-9:30, SU 11-7

Sweet Pea's Repeats

maternity

"...this is the best baby—maternity consignment store I have been to around the area... Janelle is always very helpful, and ready to look for anything you might need... very clean, easy to find what you like, not cluttered... even an area for the kids to play..."

Casual wear	✓	$$$	Prices
Business wear	×	5	Product availability
Intimate apparel	×	5	Customer service
Nursing wear	×	5	Decor

PASADENA—8220 RICHIE HWY (AT WATERFORD PLAZA); 410.315.7952; T-F 11-5, SA 11-4

Target

"...I was surprised at how fashionable their selection is—they carry Liz Lange and other really cute selections... the price is right—especially since you'll only be wearing these clothes for a few months... great for maternity basics—T-shirts, skirts, sweaters, even maternity bras... best of all, you can do some maternity shopping while you're shopping for other household basics... shirts for $10—you can't beat that... not the most exciting or romantic maternity shopping, but once you see the prices you'll get over it... as always, Target provides the perfectly priced solution..."

Casual wear	✓	$$	Prices
Business wear	✓	3	Product availability
Intimate apparel	✓	3	Customer service
Nursing wear	✓	3	Decor

WWW.TARGET.COM

GLEN BURNIE—7951 NOLPARK CT (AT NOLPARK RD); 410.969.2257; M-SA 8-10, SU 8-9; PARKING LOT IN FRONT OF STORE

East of Baltimore

"lila picks"

★Old Navy

JCPenney

"...competitive prices and a surprisingly cute selection... they carry bigger sizes that are very hard to find at other stores... much cheaper than most maternity boutiques and they always seem to have some sort of sale going on... an especially large selection of maternity jeans for plus sizes... a more conservative collection than the smaller, hipper boutiques... good for casual basics, but not much for special occasions..."

Casual wear	✓	$$	Prices
Business wear	✓	❸	Product availability
Intimate apparel	✓	❸	Customer service
Nursing wear	×	❸	Decor

WWW.JCPENNEY.COM

WHITE MARSH—8200 PERRY HALL BLVD (AT WHITE MARSH BLVD); 410.931.7550; M-TH 10-9:30, F 10-10, SA 9-10, SU 11-7; LOT

Macy's

"...if your local Macy's has a maternity section, you're in luck—call ahead!.. I bought my entire pregnancy work wardrobe at Macy's... the styles are all relatively recent and the brands are well known... you can generally find some attractive dresses at very reasonable prices on their sales rack... like other large department stores, you're bound to find something that works if you dig enough... very convenient because you can get your other shopping done at the same time... the selection isn't huge, but what they have is nice..."

Casual wear	✓	$$$	Prices
Business wear	✓	❸	Product availability
Intimate apparel	✓	❸	Customer service
Nursing wear	×	❸	Decor

WWW.MACYS.COM

PERRY HALL—8200 PERRY HALL BLVD (AT WHITE MARSH MALL); 410.931.7000; M-SA 10-9:30, SU 11-6; LOT

Motherhood Maternity

"...a wide variety of styles, from business to weekend wear—all at a good price... affordable and cute... everything from bras and swimsuits to work outfits... highly recommended for those who don't want to spend a fortune on maternity clothes... less fancy and pricey than their sister stores—A Pea in the Pod and Mimi Maternity... they have frequent sales, so you just need to keep dropping in—you're bound to find something good..."

Casual wear	✓	$$$	Prices
Business wear	✓	❹	Product availability
Intimate apparel	✓	❹	Customer service

Nursing wear ✓ — ❸ Decor

WWW.MOTHERHOOD.COM

WHITE MARSH—8200 PERRY HALL BLVD (AT WHITE MARSH MALL); 410.931.8640; M-SA 10-9:30, SU 11-6

Old Navy

"...the best for casual maternity clothing like stretchy T-shirts with Lycra and comfy jeans... prices are so reasonable it's ridiculous... not much for the workplace, but you can't beat the prices on casual ware... not all Old Navy locations carry their maternity line... don't expect a huge or diverse selection... the staff is not always knowledgeable about maternity clothing and can't really help with questions about sizing... they have the best return policy—order online and return to the nearest store location... perfect for inexpensive maternity duds..."

Casual wear	✓	$$	Prices
Business wear	✗	❹	Product availability
Intimate apparel	✗	❸	Customer service
Nursing wear	✗	❸	Decor

WWW.OLDNAVY.COM

WHITE MARSH—8123 HONEYGO BLVD (AT WHITE MARSH MALL); 410.933.3650; M-SA 9-9, SU 10-6; PARKING LOT AT MALL

Online

"lila picks"

★breastisbest.com ★gap.com

★maternitymall.com ★naissancematernity.com

babiesrus.com ★★★★☆

"...their online store is surprisingly plentiful for maternity wear in addition to all of the baby stuff... they carry everything from Mimi Maternity to Belly Basics... easy shopping and good return policy... the price is right and the selection is really good..."

Casual wear ✓ ✓ Nursing wear
Business wear ✓ ✓ Intimate apparel

babycenter.com ★★★★☆

"...it's babycenter.com—of course it's good... a small but well selected maternity section... I love being able to read other people's comments before purchasing... prices are reasonable and the convenience is priceless... great customer service and easy returns..."

Casual wear ✓ ✓ Nursing wear
Business wear ✗ ✗ Intimate apparel

babystyle.com ★★★★☆

"...beautiful selection of maternity clothes... very trendy, fashionable styles... take advantage of their free shipping offers to keep the cost down... items generally ship quickly... I found a formal maternity outfit for a benefit dinner, bought it on sale and received it on time... a nice variety of things and they ship in a timely manner..."

Casual wear ✓ ✓ Nursing wear
Business wear ✓ ✓ Intimate apparel

bellablumaternity.com

Casual wear ✓ ✓ Nursing wear
Business wear ✓ ✓ Intimate apparel

breakoutbras.com

Casual wear ✗ ✓ Nursing wear
Business wear ✗ ✓ Intimate apparel

breastisbest.com ★★★★★

"...by far the best resource for purchasing good quality nursing bras online... the site is easy to use and they have an extensive online fitting guide... returns are a breeze... since they are only online you may have to try a few before you get it exactly right..."

Casual wear ✓ ✓ Nursing wear
Business wear ✗ ✓ Intimate apparel

childishclothing.com

Casual wear ✓ ✗ Nursing wear
Business wear ✗ ✗ Intimate apparel

duematernity.com ★★★★☆

"...refreshing styles... fun and hip clothing... the site is easy to navigate and use... I've ordered a bunch of clothes from them and never had a problem... everything from casual wear to fun, funky items for special occasions... prices are reasonable..."

Casual wear ✓ ✓ Nursing wear
Business wear ✓ ✓ Intimate apparel

evalillian.com

Casual wear ✓ ✓ Nursing wear
Business wear ✓ ✓ Intimate apparel

expressiva.com ★★★★½

"...the best site for nursing clothes... prices are good and their selection is terrific... lots of selection on dressy, casual, sleep, workout and even bathing suits... if you're going to shop for maternity online then be sure not to miss this cool site... good customer service—quite prompt in answering questions about my order..."

Casual wear ✓ ✓ Nursing wear
Business wear ✗ ✓ Intimate apparel

gap.com ★★★★★

"...stylish maternity clothes delivered right to your doorstep... always something worth buying... the best place for functional, comfortable and affordable maternity clothes... classic styles, not too trendy... more available online than in a store... no fancy dresses but lots of casual outfits that are cheap, look good and I don't mind parting with them after my baby is born... easy to use site and deliveries are generally prompt... you can return them to any Gap store..."

Casual wear ✓ ✓ Nursing wear
Business wear ✓ ✓ Intimate apparel

japaneseweekend.com ★★★★☆

"...pregnancy clothes that scream 'I am proud of my pregnant body'... a must for comfy, stylish stuff... they make the best maternity pants which cradle your belly as it grows... a little expensive but I lived in their pants my entire pregnancy—I definitely got my money's worth... really nice clothing that just doesn't look and feel like your traditional pregnancy wear—I still wear a couple of the outfits (my baby is now 6 months old)..."

Casual wear ✓ ✓ Nursing wear
Business wear ✓ ✓ Intimate apparel

jcpenney.com ★★★☆☆

"...competitive prices and a surprisingly cute selection... they carry bigger sizes that are very hard to find at other stores... much cheaper than most maternity boutiques and they always seem to have some sort of sale going on... an especially large selection of maternity jeans for plus sizes... a more conservative collection than the smaller, hipper boutiques... good for casual basics, but not much for special occasions..."

Casual wear ✓ ✓ Nursing wear
Business wear ✓ ✓ Intimate apparel

lizlange.com ★★★★½

"...well-designed and cute... the real buys on this site are definitely in the sale section... cute, hip selection of jeans, skirts, blouses and

bathing suits... their evening and dressy clothes are the best with wonderful fabrics and designs... easy and convenient online shopping... practical but not frumpy styles—their web site made my maternity shopping so easy... ”

Casual wear .... ✓ ✗ .... Nursing wear
Business wear .... ✓ ✗ .... Intimate apparel

maternitymall.com ★★★★★

“*...I had great luck with maternitymall.com... a large selection of vendors in all price ranges... quick and easy without having to leave my house... found everything I needed... their merchandise tends to be true to size... site is a bit hard to navigate and cluttered with ads... sale and clearance prices are fantastic...* ”

Casual wear .... ✓ ✓ .... Nursing wear
Business wear .... ✓ ✓ .... Intimate apparel

mommygear.com

Casual wear .... ✓ ✓ .... Nursing wear
Business wear .... ✗ ✓ .... Intimate apparel

momsnightout.com

“*...for that fashionable-not-frumpy fancy occasion dress... beautiful store with gorgeous selection of dresses from cocktail to bridal... one on one attention... expensive but worth it...* ”

Casual wear .... ✗ ✗ .... Nursing wear
Business wear .... ✓ ✗ .... Intimate apparel

motherhood.com ★★★★☆

“*...a wide variety of styles, from business to weekend wear—all at a good price... affordable and cute... everything from bras and swimsuits to work outfits... highly recommended for those who don't want to spend a fortune on maternity clothes... less fancy and pricey than their sister stores—A Pea in the Pod and Mimi Maternity... they have frequent sales, so you just need to keep dropping in—you're bound to find something good...* ”

Casual wear .... ✓ ✓ .... Nursing wear
Business wear .... ✓ ✓ .... Intimate apparel

motherwear.com ★★★★½

“*...excellent selection of cute and practical nursing clothes at reasonable prices... sign up for their e-mail newsletter for great offers, including free shipping... top quality clothes... decent selection of hard to find plus sizes... golden return policy, you can return any item (even used!) you aren't 100% happy with... they sell the only nursing tops I could actually wear outside the house... cute styles that aren't frumpy... so easy... pricey but worth it for the quality... top notch customer service...* ”

Casual wear .... ✗ ✓ .... Nursing wear
Business wear .... ✗ ✓ .... Intimate apparel

naissancematernity.com ★★★★★

“*...the cutest maternity clothes around... hip and funky clothes for the artsy, well-dressed mom to be... their site is easy to navigate... if you can't make it down to the actual store in LA, just go online... clothes that make you look and feel sexy... it ain't cheap but you will look marvelous and the clothes will grow with you... web site is great and their phone order service was incredible...* ”

Casual wear .... ✓ ✗ .... Nursing wear
Business wear .... ✓ ✗ .... Intimate apparel

nordstrom.com

"...now that they don't carry maternity in stores anymore, this is the only way to get any maternity from Nordstrom... overpriced but nice... makes returns harder, since you have to ship everything instead of just going back to a store... they carry Cadeau, Liz Lange, Belly Basics, etc... nice stuff, not so nice prices..."

Casual wear	✓	✓	Nursing wear
Business wear	✓	✓	Intimate apparel

oldnavy.com

★★★★☆

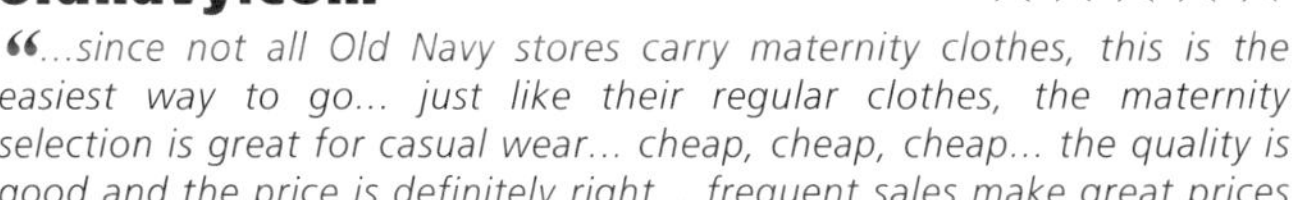

"...since not all Old Navy stores carry maternity clothes, this is the easiest way to go... just like their regular clothes, the maternity selection is great for casual wear... cheap, cheap, cheap... the quality is good and the price is definitely right... frequent sales make great prices even better..."

Casual wear	✓	✓	Nursing wear
Business wear	✗	✗	Intimate apparel

onehotmama.com

★★★½☆

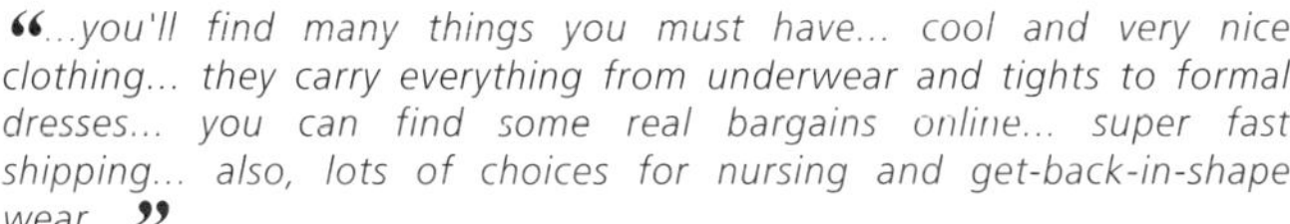

"...you'll find many things you must have... cool and very nice clothing... they carry everything from underwear and tights to formal dresses... you can find some real bargains online... super fast shipping... also, lots of choices for nursing and get-back-in-shape wear..."

Casual wear	✓	✓	Nursing wear
Business wear	✓	✓	Intimate apparel

showeryourbaby.com

Casual wear	✓	✓	Nursing wear
Business wear	✗	✓	Intimate apparel

target.com

"...lots of Liz Lange at very fair prices... the selection is great and it's so easy to shop online—we bought most of our baby gear here and I managed to slip in a couple of orders for some maternity wear too... maternity shirts for $10—where else can you find deals like that..."

Casual wear	✓	✓	Nursing wear
Business wear	✓	✓	Intimate apparel

activities & outings

Baltimore City

"lila picks"

★National Aquarium In Baltimore

★Port Discovery Children's Museum

Amazing Glaze

"...a wonderful rainy day activity for older kids... a fun birthday party, but keep in mind there isn't that much for the really little ones to do... my daughter splotched some paint on a mug and it's now her dad's favorite coffee mug... we gave some gift certificates out to friends and they still talk about the good time they had..."

Customer service........................ ❺ $$$..................................... Prices

Age range..................... 2 yrs and up

BALTIMORE—1340 SMITH AVE (AT FALLS RD); 410.532.3144; CALL FOR SCHEDULE; PARKING LOT

B&O Railroad Museum

"...every little boy's dream—steam engines and trains galore... my kids weren't too excited to go to a 'museum', but they loved it when we got there... some may be disappointed that there are only a few trains you can actually climb on... $14 for adults; 2 and under are free..."

Customer service........................ ❹ $$.. Prices

Age range..................... 2 yrs and up

WWW.BORAIL.ORG

BALTIMORE—901 W PRATT ST (AT POPPLETON ST); 410.752.2490; M-F 10-4, SA 10-5, SU 12-5; FREE PARKING

Ballet Petite

"...perfect for little girls... all sorts of classes that touch on a little girl's desire to be a princess... ballet, music, fairy tales and imagination... mommy and me dance classes... I love how they incorporate fairy tales into their classes—my daughter is totally enthralled... the end-of season recitals are priceless..."

Customer service........................ ❸ $$.. Prices

Age range..................... 2 yrs and up

WWW.BALLETPETITE.COM

BALTIMORE—4615 ROLAND AVE (AT KIRKWOOD RD); 866.738.4831; CHECK SCHEDULE ONLINE

Baltimore Museum Of Art

"...families really enjoy the extended evening hours where you can hear music, see performances, films, and do arts and crafts... tours are held every other week for preschool aged kids... perfect activity for all ages... $7 for adults; kids are free; first Thursdays of the month are free..."

Customer service........................ ❹ $$.. Prices

Age range..................... 3 yrs and up

WWW.ARTBMA.ORG

BALTIMORE—10 ART MUSEUM DR (AT N CHARLES ST); 410.396.7100; W-F 11-5, SA-SU 11-6; METERED PARKING

Baltimore Zoo

"...little children love seeing the animals... not the greatest zoo around, but a great outing on a nice day... family memberships are a great deal for those who live in the area... there are some pretty steep hills which makes pushing a stroller up them difficult... food is expensive so pack a lunch or snack... be prepared to pick your child up a lot if they're in a stroller... great summer camp for the kids ..."

Customer service .... 4 $$ .... Prices

Age range ....6 mths and up

WWW.BALTIMOREZOO.ORG

BALTIMORE—1 DRUID PARK LAKE DR (AT GLENN FALLS PKWY); 410.396.7102; DAILY 10-4:30; FREE PARKING

Barnes & Noble

"...wonderful weekly story times for all ages and frequent author visits for older kids... lovely selection of books and the story times are fun and very well done... they have evening story times—we put our kids in their pjs and come here as a treat before bedtime... they read a story, and then usually have a little craft or related coloring project... times vary by location so give them a call..."

Customer service .... 4 $ .... Prices

Age range ....6 mths to 6 yrs

WWW.BARNESANDNOBLE.COM

BALTIMORE—1819 REISTERSTOWN RD (AT WOODHOLME AVE); 410.415.5758; CALL FOR SCHEDULE

BALTIMORE—601 E PRATT ST (AT S PRESIDENT ST); 410.385.1703; CALL FOR SCHEDULE; FREE PARKING

BALTIMORE—8123 HONEYGO BLVD (AT PERRY HALL BLVD); 410.933.3670; CALL FOR SCHEDULE; FREE PARKING

Borders Books

"...very popular weekly story time held in most branches (check the web site for locations and times)... call before you go since they are very popular and get extremely crowded... kids love the unique blend of songs, stories and dancing... Mr. Hatbox's appearances are a delight to everyone (unfortunately he doesn't make appearances at all locations)... large children's section is well categorized and well priced... they make it fun for young tots to browse through the board-book section by hanging toys around the shelves... the low-key cafe is a great place to have coffee with your baby and leaf through some magazines..."

Customer service .... 4 $ .... Prices

Age range ....6 mths to 6 yrs

WWW.BORDERSSTORES.COM

BALTIMORE—8200 PERRY HALL BLVD (AT HONEYGO BLVD); 410.931.7383; CALL FOR SCHEDULE

Children of the World Co-Op

"...a groovy little play area filled with toys and educational 'play things'... great fun and a good mixture of moms and caregivers... circle time is our favorite—lots of singing and stories... several annual outings... wonderful new parent community—we've made many good friends here..."

Customer service .... 3 $$$ .... Prices

WWW.COTWCOOP.ORG

BALTIMORE—4 E UNIVERSITY PKWY (AT CHARLES ST); 410.377.5900; M-F 9:30-11:30

Chuck E Cheese's

"...lots of games, rides, playrooms and very greasy food... the kids can play and eat and parents can unwind a little... a good rainy day activity... the kids love the food, but it's a bit greasy for adults... always crowded and crazy—but that's half the fun... can you ever go wrong with pizza, games and singing?.. although they do have a salad bar for adults, remember, you're not going for the food—you're going because your kids will love it... just about the easiest birthday party around—just pay money and show up..."

Customer service........................❸ $$..Prices

Age range...............12 mths to 7 yrs

WWW.CHUCKECHEESE.COM

BALTIMORE—5912 BALTIMORE NATIONAL PIKE (AT WESTVIEW MALL); 410.719.8850; SU-TH 9-10, F-SA 9-11; FREE PARKING

BALTIMORE—8354 EASTERN AVE (AT ISLAND POINT RD); 410.288.9393; SU-TH 9-10, F-SA 9-11; FREE PARKING

Enoch Pratt Free Library

"...not just a neat collection of children's books, they also have wonderful story times... staff are great and interactive with the kids... great for a half hour of singing... Mother Goose is on the loose here... so much fun..."

Customer service........................❺ $ ....Prices

Age range...............6 mths to 12 yrs

WWW.EPFL.NET

BALTIMORE—400 CATHEDRAL ST (AT MULBERRY ST); 410.396.5430; M-W 10-8, TH 10-5:30, F-SA 10-5, SU 1-5; STREET PARKING

Inner Harbor

"...nothing specific to do, but a fun place to walk and people watch... my kids are fascinated by the boats , people and shops... not the safest place to be in the evenings... paddle boats and entertainment during the spring and summer... not the greatest for little ones who are just learning how to walk since there are no railings to prevent them from falling into the water... my kids love the street actors... check out the nearby aquarium or science center..."

Customer service........................❸ $$$......................................Prices

Age range................. 3 mths and up

WWW.BALTIMORE.ORG/BALTIMORE_INNER_HARBOR.HTM

BALTIMORE—AT PRATT & LIGHT STS; 877.BALTIMORE; FREE PARKING

Jeepers

"...they have a ton of video games and a few rides—flying bananas, bumper cars, Himalaya, monkey barrels and a train... plus, a tube for climbing and crawling... you can buy a wristband for unlimited use of the rides... awesome birthday parties... the snack bar serves up pizza, hot dogs and other 'standard' amusement park fare..."

Customer service........................❸ $$..Prices

Age range................. 2 yrs to 12 yrs

WWW.JEEPERS.COM

BALTIMORE—2521 MCCLEAN BLVD (AT CLEANLEIGH DR); 410.665.0900; M-TH 11-9, F 11-10, SA 10-10, SU 11-8

Jewish Community Center

"...programs vary from facility to facility, but most JCCs have outstanding early childhood programs... everything from mom and me music classes to arts and crafts for older kids... a wonderful place to meet other parents and make new friends... class fees are cheaper (if not free) for members, but still quite a good deal for nonmembers... a superb resource for new families looking for fun..."

Customer service .... ❹ $$$ .... Prices
Age range ....3 mths and up
WWW.JCC.ORG
BALTIMORE—5700 PARK HEIGHTS AVE (AT W NORTHERN PKWY); 410.542.4900; CALL FOR SCHEDULE

Maryland Science Center ★★★★½

"...it can get pretty crowded during the cold winter months... a nice way to spend the afternoon... the Beakers Cafe can be pricey... newly remodeled with so many awesome exhibits... they have a toddler room which includes lots of climbing equipment, a baby friendly moon walk, and a nursing area... awesome indoor fun..."

Customer service .... ❹ $$$ .... Prices
Age range ....3 mths to 10 yrs
WWW.MDSCI.ORG
BALTIMORE—601 LIGHT ST (AT E LEE ST); 410.779.3371; M-F 10-5, SA 10-6, SU 11-5

Music Together ★★★★½

"...the best mom and baby classes out there... music, singing, dancing—even instruments for tots to play with... liberal make-up policy, great venues, take home books, CDs and tapes which are different each semester... it's a national franchise so instructors vary and have their own style... different age groups get mixed up which makes it a good learning experience for all involved... the highlight of our week—grandma always comes along... be prepared to have your tot sing the songs at home, in the car—everywhere..."

Customer service .... ❹ $$$ .... Prices
Age range ....2 mths to 5 yrs
WWW.MUSICTOGETHER.COM
BALTIMORE—410.825.3881; CALL FOR SCHEDULE
BALTIMORE—410.262.7165; CALL FOR SCHEDULE

National Aquarium In Baltimore ★★★★★

"...this is one of my favorite places in the area... gorgeous and incredibly well maintained... cannot bring strollers inside, but will provide child carriers and back packs at no charge... don't miss the sea horse display and the tunnel of sharks... weekdays are usually less crowded... the dolphin show is fabulous... so much fun even for the little ones... love the aquarium—better than sea world..."

Customer service .... ❹ $$$ .... Prices
Age range ....6 mths and up
WWW.AQUA.ORG
BALTIMORE—501 E PRATT ST (AT ST CHARLES ST); 410.576.3800; SA-TH 9-5, F 9-8 ; PARKING GARAGES

Northwest Ice Rink

"...nonprofit rink that does everything it can to reach out to the public... lots of public skating sessions... great place to cool off during those hot and humid summers... plenty of lessons are offered for older kids—my little tot just loves to watch... the staff is super friendly and the ice is always kept in great condition..."

Customer service .... ❹ $$ .... Prices
Age range .... 3 yrs and up
WWW.NORTHWESTICERINK.COM
BALTIMORE—5731 COTTONWORTH AVE (AT KELLY AVE); 410.433.2307; CHECK SCHEDULE ONLINE; FREE PARKING

Port Discovery Children's Museum

"...my children love it—everything from live performances and imaginative play to science and educational programs... three floors with all sorts of activities for children... there's a rope maze in the middle connecting the floors... the cooking class was a blast... a great educational outing for the kids... perfect for all ages—they have lots of different interactive exhibits that are age appropriate... be prepared for a huge crowd on $1 day... $11 for adults; under 2 are free..."

Customer service........................❹ $$$....................................Prices

Age range...............6 mths to 12 yrs

WWW.PORTDISCOVERY.ORG

BALTIMORE—35 MARKET PL (AT E LOMBARD ST); 410.727.8120; T-F 9:30-4:30, SA 10-5, SU 12-5; PARKING GARAGES

Rebounders

"...mommy and me gym classes are perfect for the little ones... great place to meet other parents and kids... my daughter has been going since she was 8-months-old and loves it... the kids have so much fun and are always laughing... gymnastics classes for older children also available..."

Customer service........................❹ $$$....................................Prices

Age range................ 6 mths to 5 yrs

WWW.REBOUNDERS.COM

BALTIMORE—6241 FALLS RD (BETWEEN CLARKVIEW & RACQUET); 410.337.7012; CHECK SCHEDULE ONLINE; PARKING LOT

Red Canoe

"...a bustling children's bookstore... they often host play groups, book discussions, writing classes and even nature walks... the first level has a play area and a cafe which serves coffee drinks, breakfast and lunch... love their book selection... a great outing with tots and a fabulous way to meet new friends..."

Customer service........................❺ $$......................................Prices

Age range................ 6 mths to 5 yrs

WWW.REDCANOE.BZ

BALTIMORE—4337 HARFORD RD (AT COLD SPRING LN); 410.444.4440; M-T 7:30-2, W-SA 7:30-5, SU 10-3; FREE PARKING

Top of the World Observation Level

"...great fun not just for tourists... my son loves going all the way up to the 27th floor and checking out the view... an easy, fun stop in town—elevator ride and beautiful view... the kind of thing that is more exciting when you do it with kids..."

Customer service........................❸ $ ....Prices

Age range.................6 mths and up

WWW.CLOISTERSCASTLE.COM/TOPTHEWORLD/TOPOFTHEWORLD.ASPX

BALTIMORE—401 E PRATT ST (AT GAY ST); 410.837.8439; W-SU 10-6; FREE PARKING

Walters Art Museum

"...amazing Chamber of Wonders where you can see paintings, sculptures, armor, bugs, beetles, butterflies, and a 12 ft long stuffed alligator... teenage docents will wow you with their knowledge of the art collection... drop in art activities are unique and fun for kids of all ages..."

Customer service........................❹ $$$....................................Prices

WWW.THEWALTERS.ORG

BALTIMORE—600 N CHARLES ST (AT E CENTRE ST); 410.547.9000; W-SU 10-5; PARKING LOT

YMCA

"...most of the Ys in the area have classes and activities for kids... swimming, gym classes, dance—even play groups for the really little ones... ... some facilities are nicer than others, but in general their programs are worth checking out... prices are more than reasonable for what is offered... the best bang for your buck... they have it all—great programs that meet the needs of a diverse range of families... check out their camps during the summer and school breaks..."

Customer service .... 4 $$ .... Prices

Age range ....3 mths and up

WWW.YMCAMD.ORG

BALTIMORE—1609 DRUID HILL AVE (AT MCMECHEN ST); 410.728.1600; M-F 6:30-10, SA 7-6, SU 12-5; FREE PARKING

North of Baltimore

"lila picks"

★Build-A-Bear Workshop

★My Gym Children's Fitness Center

Baby Boosters

"...a free service put on by the Baltimore County Public Libraries for babies... a wonderful way to introduce your baby to books, puppets, singing and more in a group setting... a great way to meet other parents..."

Customer service.......................... ❸ $ .... Prices

Age range................. 3 mths to 2 yrs

WWW.BABYBOOSTERS.ORG

TOWSON—320 YORK RD (AT BALTIMORE COUNTY PUBLIC LIBRARY); 410.887.6127; CHECK SCHEDULE ONLINE; FREE PARKING

Barnes & Noble

"...wonderful weekly story times for all ages and frequent author visits for older kids... lovely selection of books and the story times are fun and very well done... they have evening story times—we put our kids in their pjs and come here as a treat before bedtime... they read a story, and then usually have a little craft or related coloring project... times vary by location so give them a call..."

Customer service.......................... ❹ $ .... Prices

Age range................. 6 mths to 6 yrs

WWW.BARNESANDNOBLE.COM

BEL AIR—620 MARKETPLACE DR (AT BELAIR RD); 410.638.7023; CALL FOR SCHEDULE

TOWSON—1 E JOPPA RD (ACROSS FROM TOWSON TOWN CTR); 410.296.7021; CALL FOR SCHEDULE

Borders Books

"...very popular weekly story time held in most branches (check the web site for locations and times)... call before you go since they are very popular and get extremely crowded... kids love the unique blend of songs, stories and dancing... Mr. Hatbox's appearances are a delight to everyone (unfortunately he doesn't make appearances at all locations)... large children's section is well categorized and well priced... they make it fun for young tots to browse through the board-book section by hanging toys around the shelves... the low-key cafe is a great place to have coffee with your baby and leaf through some magazines..."

Customer service.......................... ❹ $ .... Prices

Age range................. 6 mths to 6 yrs

WWW.BORDERSSTORES.COM

LUTHERVILLE—170 W RIDGELY RD (AT YORK RD); CALL FOR SCHEDULE

Build-A-Bear Workshop

"...design and make your own bear—it's a dream come true... the most cherished toy my daughter owns... they even come with birth certificates... the staff is fun and knows how to play along with the kids' excitement... the basic stuffed animal is only about $15, but the extras add up quickly... great for field trips, birthdays and special occasions... how darling—my nephew is 8 years old now, and still sleeps with his favorite bear..."

Customer service .... ❹ $$$ .... Prices
Age range .... 3 yrs and up

WWW.BUILDABEAR.COM

TOWSON—825 DULANEY VALLEY RD (AT TOWSON TOWN CTR); 410.321.5958; M-SA 10-9, SU 11-6; FREE PARKING

Chuck E Cheese's

"...lots of games, rides, playrooms and very greasy food... the kids can play and eat and parents can unwind a little... a good rainy day activity... the kids love the food, but it's a bit greasy for adults... always crowded and crazy—but that's half the fun... can you ever go wrong with pizza, games and singing?.. although they do have a salad bar for adults, remember, you're not going for the food—you're going because your kids will love it... just about the easiest birthday party around—just pay money and show up..."

Customer service .... ❸ $$ .... Prices
Age range .... 12 mths to 7 yrs

WWW.CHUCKECHEESE.COM

BEL AIR—5 BEL AIR S PKWY (AT RTE 924); 410.515.0207; SU-TH 9-10, F-SA 9-11; PARKING LOT

TOWSON—809 GOUCHER BLVD (AT E JOPPA RD); 410.823.1756; SU-TH 9-10, F-SA 9-11; FREE PARKING

Fire Museum Of Maryland

"...perfect for your little firefighter... take the tour through the most historical fire truck (a horse drawn fire carriage) to the more modern... a large kids' playroom where your little one can play on a real fire truck and a wooden one and dress up in fire gear... fire engines galore... $6 for adults; under 2 is free..."

Customer service .... ❺ $$ .... Prices
Age range .... 12 mths and up

WWW.FIREMUSEUMMD.ORG

LUTHERVILLE—1301 YORK RD (AT RTE 45); 410.321.7500; T-SA 11-4

Gymboree Play & Music

"...we've done several rounds of classes with our kids and they absolutely love it... colorful, padded environment with tons of things to climb and play on... a good indoor place to meet other families and for kids to learn how to play with each other... the equipment and play areas are generally neat and clean... an easy birthday party spot... a guaranteed nap after class... costs vary, so call before showing up..."

Customer service .... ❹ $$$ .... Prices
Age range .... birth to 5 yrs

WWW.GYMBOREE.COM

PARKVILLE—8813 WALTHAM WOODS RD (AT E JOPPA RD); 410.663.0200; CHECK SCHEDULE ONLINE

TOWSON—1320 PROVIDENCE RD (AT VALEWOOD RD); 866.663.0200; CHECK SCHEDULE ONLINE; FREE PARKING

Jeepers

"...they have a ton of video games and a few rides—flying bananas, bumper cars, Himalaya, monkey barrels and a train... plus, a tube for

activities & outings

climbing and crawling... you can buy a wristband for unlimited use of the rides... awesome birthday parties... the snack bar serves up pizza, hot dogs and other 'standard' amusement park fare... ❞

Customer service.........................❸ $$..Prices
Age range.................. 2 yrs to 12 yrs

WWW.JEEPERS.COM

PARKVILLE—700 HUNGERFORD DR (AT A ST); 301.309.2525; M-TH 11-9, F 11-10, SA 10-10, SU 11-8

Kindermusik ★★★★☆

❝*...a wonderful intro to music and group play... well-trained professionals make it both educational and fun for all ages... we started with the mom & baby class and now my boy feels confident enough to play without me... they have hundreds of programs nationwide... class quality definitely varies from location to location, and teacher to teacher... different classes for different ages... singing, movement, dancing and rhythm—what's not to like?...* ❞

Customer service.........................❹ $$$......................................Prices
Age range................. 2 mths to 7 yrs

WWW.KINDERMUSIK.COM

HUNT VALLEY—717.993.3779; CALL FOR SCHEDULE

My Gym Children's Fitness Center ★★★★★

❝*...a wonderful gym environment for parents with babies and older tots... classes range from tiny tots to school-aged children and the staff is great about making it fun for all ages... equipment and facilities are really neat—ropes, pulleys, swings, you name it... the kind of place your kids hate to leave... the staff's enthusiasm is contagious... great for memorable birthday parties... although it's a franchise, each gym seems to have its own individual feeling... awesome for meeting playmates and other parents...* ❞

Customer service.........................❹ $$$......................................Prices
Age range.................. 3 mths to 9 yrs

WWW.MY-GYM.COM

BEL AIR—1206 AGORA DR (AT AMYCLAE PL); 410.838.3042; CHECK SCHEDULE ONLINE

TIMONIUM—2080 YORK RD (OFF RTE 45); 410.308.1288; CHECK SCHEDULE ONLINE; FREE PARKING

Padonia Park Club ★★★★½

❝*...beautiful outdoor pools... great place to join as a family... the park has two baby pools and one children's pool... my girls love it here... playground, sports facilities, nature trail, paddle boating, swim lessons, and more... great summer activities...* ❞

Customer service.........................❺ $$$......................................Prices
Age range.................. 3 mths and up

WWW.PADONIAPARKCLUB.COM

COCKEYSVILLE—12006 JENIFER RD (AT YORK RD); 410.252.2046; M-F 9-5; PARKING LOT

Rebounders ★★★★☆

❝*...mommy and me gym classes are perfect for the little ones... great place to meet other parents and kids... my daughter has been going since she was 8-months-old and loves it... the kids have so much fun and are always laughing... gymnastics classes for older children also available...* ❞

Customer service.........................❹ $$$......................................Prices
Age range................6 mths to 12 yrs

WWW.REBOUNDERS.COM

TIMONIUM—7A W AYLESBURY RD (OFF RTE 45); 410.252.3374; CHECK SCHEDULE ONLINE

YMCA

"...most of the Ys in the area have classes and activities for kids... swimming, gym classes, dance—even play groups for the really little ones... ... some facilities are nicer than others, but in general their programs are worth checking out... prices are more than reasonable for what is offered... the best banq for your buck... they have it all—great programs that meet the needs of a diverse range of families... check out their camps during the summer and school breaks..."

Customer service .... ❹ $$ .... Prices

Age range ....3 mths and up

WWW.YMCAMD.ORG

TOWSON—600 W CHESAPEAKE AVE (AT DIXIE DR); 410.823.8870; M-F 5:30-10, SA 7-8, SU 8-8; FREE PARKING

West of Baltimore

"lila picks"

★Gymboree Play & Music

★My Gym Children's Fitness Center

Borders Books

"...very popular weekly story time held in most branches (check the web site for locations and times)... call before you go since they are very popular and get extremely crowded... kids love the unique blend of songs, stories and dancing... Mr. Hatbox's appearances are a delight to everyone (unfortunately he doesn't make appearances at all locations)... large children's section is well categorized and well priced... they make it fun for young tots to browse through the board-book section by hanging toys around the shelves... the low-key cafe is a great place to have coffee with your baby and leaf through some magazines..."

Customer service........................❹ $ .... Prices

Age range................ 6 mths to 6 yrs

WWW.BORDERSSTORES.COM

OWINGS MILLS—10300 MILL RUN CIR (AT RED RUN BLVD); 410.363.7510; CALL FOR SCHEDULE

Gymboree Play & Music

"...we've done several rounds of classes with our kids and they absolutely love it... colorful, padded environment with tons of things to climb and play on... a good indoor place to meet other families and for kids to learn how to play with each other... the equipment and play areas are generally neat and clean... an easy birthday party spot... a guaranteed nap after class... costs vary, so call before showing up..."

Customer service........................❹ $$$..................................... Prices

Age range....................birth to 5 yrs

WWW.GYMBOREE.COM

OWINGS MILLS—10999 RED RUN BLVD (AT PLEASANT HILLS CTR); 866.663.0200; CHECK SCHEDULE ONLINE; FREE PARKING

Jewish Community Center

"...programs vary from facility to facility, but most JCCs have outstanding early childhood programs... everything from mom and me music classes to arts and crafts for older kids... a wonderful place to meet other parents and make new friends... class fees are cheaper (if not free) for members, but still quite a good deal for nonmembers... a superb resource for new families looking for fun..."

Customer service........................❹ $$$..................................... Prices

Age range................. 3 mths and up

WWW.JCC.ORG

OWINGS MILLS—3506 GWYNNBROOK AVE (AT GARRISON FOREST RD); 410.356.5200; CHECK SCHEDULE ONLINE

Miss Iris and Miss Anne's Totland

"...Miss Anne and Miss Iris are wonderful... the kids really love the singing, dancing and activities... classes are for infants to age three... classes are age appropriate... babies go nuts over these classes... a bit pricey... kids love Miss Anne's birthday parties... the teachers are very personable and remember all of the kids after the first couple classes...."

Customer service .... ❺ $$$ .... Prices
Age range .... 3 mths to 3 yrs

REISTERSTOWN—410.833.1396; CALL FOR SCHEDULE; STREET PARKING

Music Together

"...the best mom and baby classes out there... music, singing, dancing—even instruments for tots to play with... liberal make-up policy, great venues, take home books, CDs and tapes which are different each semester... it's a national franchise so instructors vary and have their own style... different age groups get mixed up which makes it a good learning experience for all involved... the highlight of our week—grandma always comes along... be prepared to have your tot sing the songs at home, in the car—everywhere..."

Customer service .... ❹ $$$ .... Prices
Age range .... 2 mths to 5 yrs

WWW.MUSICTOGETHER.COM

CATONSVILLE—110 N BEECHWOOD AVE (AT SUMMIT AVE); 410.747.4957; CALL FOR SCHEDULE

OWINGS MILLS—410.654.6423; CALL FOR SCHEDULE

My Gym Children's Fitness Center

"...a wonderful gym environment for parents with babies and older tots... classes range from tiny tots to school-aged children and the staff is great about making it fun for all ages... equipment and facilities are really neat—ropes, pulleys, swings, you name it... the kind of place your kids hate to leave... the staff's enthusiasm is contagious... great for memorable birthday parties... although it's a franchise, each gym seems to have its own individual feeling... awesome for meeting playmates and other parents..."

Customer service .... ❹ $$$ .... Prices
Age range .... 3 mths to 9 yrs

WWW.MY-GYM.COM

OWINGS MILLS—9419 COMMON BROOK RD (AT LAKESIDE BLVD); 410.654.7575; CHECK SCHEDULE ONLINE; FREE PARKING

YMCA

"...most of the Ys in the area have classes and activities for kids... swimming, gym classes, dance—even play groups for the really little ones... ... some facilities are nicer than others, but in general their programs are worth checking out... prices are more than reasonable for what is offered... the best bang for your buck... they have it all—great programs that meet the needs of a diverse range of families... check out their camps during the summer and school breaks..."

Customer service .... ❹ $$ .... Prices
Age range .... 3 mths and up

WWW.YMCAMD.ORG

CATONSVILLE—850 S ROLLING RD (AT CAMPUS DR); 410.747.9622; M-F 5:30-9:45, SA 7-6:45, SU 10-6:45; FREE PARKING

South of Baltimore

"lila picks"

★ Chesapeake Children's Museum

★ Gymboree Play & Music

Barnes & Noble

"...wonderful weekly story times for all ages and frequent author visits for older kids... lovely selection of books and the story times are fun and very well done... they have evening story times—we put our kids in their pjs and come here as a treat before bedtime... they read a story, and then usually have a little craft or related coloring project... times vary by location so give them a call..."

Customer service........................❹ $ .... Prices

Age range................ 6 mths to 6 yrs

WWW.BARNESANDNOBLE.COM

ANNAPOLIS—2516 SOLOMON'S ISLAND RD (AT ARRIS T ALLEN BLVD); 410.573.1115; CALL FOR SCHEDULE; FREE PARKING

Borders Books

"...very popular weekly story time held in most branches (check the web site for locations and times)... call before you go since they are very popular and get extremely crowded... kids love the unique blend of songs, stories and dancing... Mr. Hatbox's appearances are a delight to everyone (unfortunately he doesn't make appearances at all locations)... large children's section is well categorized and well priced... they make it fun for young tots to browse through the board-book section by hanging toys around the shelves... the low-key cafe is a great place to have coffee with your baby and leaf through some magazines..."

Customer service........................❹ $ .... Prices

Age range................ 6 mths to 6 yrs

WWW.BORDERSSTORES.COM

ANNAPOLIS—1115 ANNAPOLIS MALL (OFF DEFENSE HWY); 410.571.0923; CALL FOR SCHEDULE

GLEN BURNIE—7900 RITCHIE HWY (AT MARLEY STATION SHOPPING CTR); 410.760.5733; CALL FOR SCHEDULE

Build-A-Bear Workshop

"...design and make your own bear—it's a dream come true... the most cherished toy my daughter owns... they even come with birth certificates... the staff is fun and knows how to play along with the kids' excitement... the basic stuffed animal is only about $15, but the extras add up quickly... great for field trips, birthdays and special occasions... how darling—my nephew is 8 years old now, and still sleeps with his favorite bear..."

Customer service........................❹ $$$..................................... Prices

Age range....................3 yrs and up

WWW.BUILDABEAR.COM

ANNAPOLIS—1800 ANNAPOLIS MALL (AT BESTGATE RD); 410.897.0828; M-SA 10-9:30, SU 11-6; MALL PARKING

Chesapeake Children's Museum

"...an inexpensive way to spend the afternoon with your toddler or preschooler... turtles, snakes, dress up, art projects and blocks are just some of the hands-on activities... check out the new NASA 'sun' exhibit... my kids love exploring the different exhibits... there is always something new to see and learn... visitors can travel the world once they enter the museum doors, a rotating exhibit features a different country or culture every few months... $3 for ages 1 and up..."

Customer service .... ❸ $ .... Prices
Age range ....6 mths and up

WWW.THECCM.ORG

ANNAPOLIS—25 SILOPANNA RD (AT SPA DR); 410.990.1993; DAILY 10-4

Chuck E Cheese's

"...lots of games, rides, playrooms and very greasy food... the kids can play and eat and parents can unwind a little... a good rainy day activity... the kids love the food, but it's a bit greasy for adults... always crowded and crazy—but that's half the fun... can you ever go wrong with pizza, games and singing?.. although they do have a salad bar for adults, remember, you're not going for the food—you're going because your kids will love it... just about the easiest birthday party around—just pay money and show up..."

Customer service .... ❸ $$ .... Prices
Age range .... 12 mths to 7 yrs

WWW.CHUCKECHEESE.COM

ANNAPOLIS—2333-A FOREST DR (AT OLD SOLOMONS ISLAND RD); 410.266.1438; SU-TH 9-10, F-SA 9-11; FREE PARKING

GLEN BURNIE—6637 GOVERNOR RITCHIE HWY (AT GLEN BURNIE MALL); 410.761.3131; SU-TH 9-10, F-SA 9-11; FREE PARKING

Gymboree Play & Music

"...we've done several rounds of classes with our kids and they absolutely love it... colorful, padded environment with tons of things to climb and play on... a good indoor place to meet other families and for kids to learn how to play with each other... the equipment and play areas are generally neat and clean... an easy birthday party spot... a guaranteed nap after class... costs vary, so call before showing up..."

Customer service .... ❹ $$$ .... Prices
Age range .... birth to 5 yrs

WWW.GYMBOREE.COM

MILLERSVILLE—1114 BENFIELD BLVD (AT NAJOLES RD); 866.663.0200; CHECK SCHEDULE ONLINE; FREE PARKING

Kindermusik

"...a wonderful intro to music and group play... well-trained professionals make it both educational and fun for all ages... we started with the mom & baby class and now my boy feels confident enough to play without me... they have hundreds of programs nationwide... class quality definitely varies from location to location, and teacher to teacher... different classes for different ages... singing, movement, dancing and rhythm—what's not to like?..."

Customer service .... ❹ $$$ .... Prices
Age range ....2 mths to 7 yrs

WWW.KINDERMUSIK.COM

GLEN BURNIE—410.969.7597

Little Gym, The

"...a well thought-out program of gym and tumbling geared toward different age groups... a clean facility, excellent and knowledgeable staff... we love the small-sized gym equipment and their willingness to work with kids with special needs... activities are fun and personalized to match the kids' age... great place for birthday parties with a nice party room—they'll organize and do everything for you..."

Customer service........................❹ $$$.......................................Prices

Age range...............4 mths to 12 yrs

WWW.THELITTLEGYM.COM

SEVERNA PARK—558 RITCHIE HWY (AT ROBINSON RD); 410.544.3800; CALL FOR SCHEDULE; FREE PARKING

Music Together

"...the best mom and baby classes out there... music, singing, dancing—even instruments for tots to play with... liberal make-up policy, great venues, take home books, CDs and tapes which are different each semester... it's a national franchise so instructors vary and have their own style... different age groups get mixed up which makes it a good learning experience for all involved... the highlight of our week—grandma always comes along... be prepared to have your tot sing the songs at home, in the car—everywhere..."

Customer service........................❹ $$$.......................................Prices

Age range................ 2 mths to 5 yrs

WWW.MUSICTOGETHER.COM

CROFTON—301.262.9538; CALL FOR SCHEDULE

EDGEWATER—301.262.9538; CALL FOR SCHEDULE

SEVERNA PARK—301.262.9538; CALL FOR SCHEDULE

East of Baltimore

Reel Moms (Loews Theatres)

"...not really an activity for kids, but rather something you can easily do with your baby... first-run movies for people with babies... the sound is low, the lights turned up and no one cares if your baby cries... packed with moms changing diapers all over the place... so nice to be able to go see current movies... don't have to worry about baby noise... relaxed environment with moms, dads and babies wandering all over... the staff is very friendly and there is a real community feel... a great idea and very well done..."

Customer service .... ❹ $$ .... Prices
Age range .... 3 mths to 2 yrs

WWW.ENJOYTHESHOW.COM/REELMOMS

WHITE MARSH—8141 HONEYGO BLVD (AT WHITE MARSH MALL); 410.933.9034; CHECK SCHEDULE ONLINE; PARKING IN FRONT OF BLDG

parks & playgrounds

Baltimore City

"lila picks"

★Federal Hill Park

★Meadowhood Regional Park

Druid Hill Park

★★★★☆

"...a huge park that has tennis courts, Baltimore City mock traffic course for children, a lake reservoir, and more... the largest park in Baltimore city... the zoo and the Druid Park Conservatory is also in the park..."

Equipment/play structures........... ❹ ❸ .... Maintenance

WWW.CI.BALTIMORE.MD.US

BALTIMORE—2600 MADISON AVE (AT SWANN DR); 410.396.6106

Federal Hill Park

★★★★★

"...sometimes needs a little TLC, but a great neighborhood park... nice park with a great view... the equipment is nice... area is fenced in and dog free... if you live downtown, this park will be your mainstay... a beautiful park in the middle of the city... climbers, swings, area for jogging or walking..."

Equipment/play structures........... ❹ ❹ .... Maintenance

WWW.MYTRAVELGUIDE.COM/ATTRACTIONS/PROFILE-79735805-UNITED_STATES_MARYLAND_BALTIMORE_FEDERAL_HILL_PARK.HTML

BALTIMORE—800 BATTERY AVE (AT KEY HWY); 410.396.5828

Hannah Moore Park

★★★★★

"...best park for kids of all ages... toddler lot, sand box, elementary equiplment, bike / skate path... this park is great, not one thing to complain about..."

Equipment/play structures........... ❺ ❺ .... Maintenance

WWW.CI.BALTIMORE.MD.US

BALTIMORE—REISTERSTOWN RD (AT MENLO DR)

Meadowood Regional Park

★★★★★

"...this park is huge and perfect for riding bikes, roller skates, or scooters... covered picnic tables for parties, playgroups or just lunch... two main areas with playground equipment—one for toddlers and the other for bigger children... very clean and great for strollers, walking, and picnicking ..."

Equipment/play structures........... ❺ ❺ .... Maintenance

WWW.CO.BA.MD.US/AGENCIES/RECREATION/COUNTYPARKS/CTYPARKSLIST.HTML

BALTIMORE—10650 FALLS RD (OFF JONES FALLS PKWY); 410.887.3678

Patterson Park

★★★½☆

"...we are anxiously awaiting the great new playground they're building... love feeding the ducks... also an outdoor pool... love all the

history there, and the the ice skating... they could do a better job picking up trash... ❞

Equipment/play structures .... ❸ ❸ .... Maintenance

WWW.PATTERSONPARK.COM

BALTIMORE—LINWOOD AVE (AT EASTERN AVE); 410.276.3676

Reisterstown Regional Park ★★★☆☆

❝*...a great place and never crowded... picnic tables under a pavilion make it a nice place to picnic... also ball fields, restrooms, and a nice playground...* ❞

Equipment/play structures .... ❹ ❹ .... Maintenance

WWW.CO.BA.MD.US/AGENCIES/RECREATION/COUNTYPARKS/CTYPARKSLIST.HTML

BALTIMORE—401 MITCHELL DR (AT E RIVERSIDE AVE); 410.887.1163

Sherwood Gardens ★★★★☆

❝*...no playground facilities, but great for a picnic or just running around... in a quiet, quaint neighborhood... tulips in the spring are amazing!...* ❞

Equipment/play structures .... ❸ ❸ .... Maintenance

WWW.MDISFUN.ORG/HOME/INDEX.ASP

BALTIMORE—4100 GREENWAY ST (AT HIGHFIELD RD); 410.323.7982

Wyman Park ★★★★☆

❝*...new (3 years old) playground equipment, very good for toddlers... community feeling... not a tremendous amount of stuff, but a nice place to come and play if you live nearby...* ❞

Equipment/play structures .... ❹ ❹ .... Maintenance

WWW.CI.BALTIMORE.MD.US/GOVERNMENT/RECNPARKS

BALTIMORE—34TH ST (OFF RT 95)

North of Baltimore

"lila picks"

★Rodgers Forge Tot Lot

Double Rock Park ★★★★☆

"...nice playgrounds and wonderful walking paths... little waterfalls and stones in the creek for the kids to play with... plenty of grills and picnic areas, ball fields, and restrooms... limited parking and the playground is a little outdated..."

Equipment/play structures........... ❹ ❸ ....Maintenance

WWW.CO.BA.MD.US/AGENCIES/RECREATION/COUNTYPARKS/CTYPARKSLIST.HTML

PARKVILLE—8211 TEXAS AVE (AT AVONDALE RD); 410.887.5300

Oregon Ridge Park ★★★★½

"...a pond with a beach!... nice, but there aren't any bathrooms available... fun learning center with bookstore for the kids... employees take time to talk to guests and educate kids... during summer swimming also available..."

Equipment/play structures........... ❺ ❺ ....Maintenance

WWW.CO.BA.MD.US/AGENCIES/RECREATION/COUNTYPARKS/CTYPARKSLIST.HTML

COCKEYSVILLE—13555 BEAVER DAM RD (AT SHAWAN RD); 410.887.1818

Putty Hill Park ★★★½☆

"...pavilion, picnic area, playground, ball field, restrooms, and courts... very large 14 acre park... wonderful area for the kids to play..."

Equipment/play structures........... ❸ ❸ ....Maintenance

WWW.CO.BA.MD.US/AGENCIES/RECREATION/COUNTYPARKS/CTYPARKSLIST.HTML

PARKVILLE—8600 HOERNER RD (AT PUTTY HILL AVE); 410.887.5300

Rodgers Forge Tot Lot ★★★★★

"...this is a great park for all ages... lots to do for the little ones... a huge sand box with shovels, pails, construction trucks, wheelbarrow etc... all around the park there are big plastic cars, bikes, and other riding toys for children to use as well as the normal swings, slides, and climbing structures... most equipment I've ever seen!..."

Equipment/play structures........... ❺ ❺ ....Maintenance

WWW.CI.BALTIMORE.MD.US/GOVERNMENT/RECNPARKS/HOME.HTM

TOWSON—YORK RD (AT BELLONA AVE); 410.396.7458

West of Baltimore

Bloomsbury Community Center

"...great spacious twelve acres, with a community center, tennis courts, ball fields, and restrooms..."

Equipment/play structures .... ❸ ❸ .... Maintenance

WWW.CO.BA.MD.US/AGENCIES/RECREATION/COUNTYPARKS/CTYPARKSLIST.HTML

CATONSVILLE—106 BLOOMSBURY AVE (AT BLOOMINGDALE AVE); 410.887.0959

Hannah More Park

"...a huge park, but quite crowded on evenings and weekends... wonderful park for kids of all ages... always clean and well maintained... lots of stuff for the kids to do..."

Equipment/play structures .... ❺ ❺ .... Maintenance

WWW.CO.BA.MD.US/AGENCIES/RECREATION/COUNTYPARKS/CTYPARKSLIST.HTML

REISTERSTOWN—12035 REISTERSTOWN RD (AT E CHERRY HILL RD); 410.887.1142

Lurman Woodland Theatre

"...easy to bring kids here, bring a blanket to sit on, food, and enjoy the music... amphitheater, nature trails and restrooms..."

Equipment/play structures .... ❸ ❹ .... Maintenance

WWW.CO.BA.MD.US/AGENCIES/RECREATION/COUNTYPARKS/CTYPARKSLIST.HTML

CATONSVILLE—AT HILLTOP RD (AT CATONSVILLE HIGH SCHOOL); 410.887.0959

South of Baltimore

"lila picks"

★Quiet Waters Park

Gay Oaks Park ★★★☆☆

"...a picnic area, playground, multipurpose courts... typical, decent sized park..."

Equipment/play structures........... ❸ ❸ .... Maintenance

WWW.CO.BA.MD.US/AGENCIES/RECREATION/COUNTYPARKS/CTYPARKSLIST.HTML

ARBUTUS—SURPHUR SPRING RD (AT DOLORES AVE); 410.887.1453

Halethorpe Community Center ★★★½☆

"...a community center, pavilion, picnic area, playground, ball field, restrooms, and courts... a nice little park..."

Equipment/play structures........... ❸ ❸ .... Maintenance

WWW.CO.BA.MD.US/AGENCIES/RECREATION/COUNTYPARKS/CTYPARKSLIST.HTML

ARBUTUS—1900 NORTHEAST AVE (AT WASHINGTON BLVD); 410.887.1453

Lake Waterford Park ★★★★☆

"...I love this park!... for no admission fee, you can enjoy a huge playground, basketball courts, picnic tables, a lake, and walks through the woods... the playground has modern equipment, a recycled rubber ground, and it is designed for children from two to eleven... there is something for all of the kids... I also love taking my daughter for walks around the lake..."

Equipment/play structures........... ❹ ❹ .... Maintenance

WWW.AACOUNTY.ORG

PASADENA—E PASADENA RD (AT PENNY LN); 410.222.6248

Quiet Waters Park ★★★★★

"...beautiful park with a little something for everyone to enjoy... wonderful playground and walking trail, close to downtown Annapolis... the grounds are stunning... lots of room for the kids to run around... yearly pass is $25, buy one and go every day!..."

Equipment/play structures........... ❹ ❺ .... Maintenance

WWW.FRIENDSOFQUIETWATERSPARK.HOMESTEAD.COM/

ANNAPOLIS—HILLSMERE DR (AT QUIET WATERS PARK RD); 410.268.7866

East of Baltimore

"lila picks"

★Honeygo Run Regional Park

Cox's Point Park ★★★★☆

"...nice, quiet, relaxing... clean and great for a family cookout... feeding the ducks is always a hit with my child... pavilions, picnic area, playground, fishing, restrooms, and a boat ramp..."

Equipment/play structures .... ❹ ❹ .... Maintenance

WWW.CO.BA.MD.US/AGENCIES/RECREATION/COUNTYPARKS/CTYPARKSLIST.HTML

ESSEX—820 RIVERSIDE DR (BY DUCK CREEK); 410.887.0255

Honeygo Run Regional Park ★★★★★

"...great walking/running trail and playground... pavilions and bathroom facilities also available... nice playground. good track for walking... water fountain and picnic tables..."

Equipment/play structures .... ❺ ❺ .... Maintenance

WWW.CO.BA.MD.US/AGENCIES/RECREATION/COUNTYPARKS/CTYPARKSLIST.HTML

PERRY HALL—9033 HONEYGO BLVD (AT EBENEZER RD); 410.887.5187

Loreley Community Center

"...a nice little area with a community center, playground, ball field, courts... decent for the typical outing..."

Equipment/play structures .... ❸ ❸ .... Maintenance

WWW.CO.BA.MD.US/AGENCIES/RECREATION/COUNTYPARKS/CTYPARKSLIST.HTML

WHITE MARSH—11550 PHILADELPHIA RD (AT NEW FORGE RD); 410.887.5194

Rosedale Park

"...a nice, but small, play area for small tots at the end of the playground... while this is not a park to escape city traffic noises, it is enjoyable because of the large playing fields, ample playground equipment, easy access/location, and beach volleyball set-up (bring your own volleyball!)..."

Equipment/play structures .... ❹ ❹ .... Maintenance

WWW.CO.BA.MD.US/AGENCIES/RECREATION/COUNTYPARKS/CTYPARKSLIST.HTML

ROSEDALE—1246 KENDRICK RD (AT BERKFIELD RD); 410.887.0294

Victory Villa Community Center

"...great place for a party... lots of dances held here for older kids... should have a playground, but prices are great..."

Equipment/play structures .... ❹ ❹ .... Maintenance

WWW.CO.BA.MD.US/AGENCIES/RECREATION/COUNTYPARKS/CTYPARKSLIST.HTML

MIDDLE RIVER—404 COMPASS RD (OFF MARTIN BLVD); 410.887.0234

restaurants

Baltimore City

"lila picks"

★Panera Bread

Afghan Kabob

"...this is a fast-food Afghan restaurant... not fancy, (order at the counter, get it delivered to your table on paper plates), but it's really good... they have a vegetarian plate that is delicious... consists of rice, juicy eggplant, sweet pumpkin with yogurt and mint, pitas, a tabouleh-like salad, and an okra dish... they have highchairs, and a nice staff..."

Children's menu	✗	$	Prices
Changing station	✗	❸	Customer service
Highchairs/boosters	✓	❷	Stroller access

BALTIMORE—37 S CHARLES ST (AT LOMBARD ST); 410.727.5511; M-F 11-9, SA-SU 12-9

Amer's Café

"...this restaurant is a little out of the way, but worth the trip... kids get to make their own pizzas at the pizza counter... on Friday and Saturday nights there is Belly Dancing... with all this entertainment the adults might even get to finish a sentence..."

Children's menu	✗	$$	Prices
Changing station	✗	❺	Customer service
Highchairs/boosters	✓	❺	Stroller access

WWW.AMERSCAFE.COM

BALTIMORE—7624 BELAIR RD (AT CARDWELL AVE); 410.668.5100; T-SU 11-10, F-SA 11-11

Bill Bateman's Bistro

"...great food and great service... well done kids menu, fitting the well done lively and active bistro... don't worry about making a ruckus, or a mess here... staff is great and happily accommodates families with little children..."

Children's menu	✓	$$	Prices
Changing station	✗	❹	Customer service
Highchairs/boosters	✓	❹	Stroller access

WWW.BILLBATEMAN.COM

BALTIMORE—8810 WALTHAM WOODS RD (AT JOPPA RD); 410.668.1080; M-SA 11-2, SU 11-1; PARKING LOT

Bob Evans Farms Restaurant

"...home style cooking... worth the wait for their breakfast... arrive early to beat the weekend crowds... slings available for car seats... kid-friendly... reasonable prices... sausage, eggs and hot cakes... easy food—especially if you have picky eaters with you..."

Children's menu	✓	$$	Prices
Changing station	✓	❹	Customer service
Highchairs/boosters	✓	❹	Stroller access

WWW.BOBEVANS.COM

BALTIMORE—4110 WHOLESALE CLUB DR (AT RTE 1); 410.882.1043; DAILY 7-10; FREE PARKING

California Pizza Kitchen

"...you can't go wrong with their fabulous pizza... always clean... the food's great, the kids drinks all come with a lid... the staff is super friendly to kids... crayons and coloring books keep little minds busy... most locations have a place for strollers at the front... no funny looks or attitude when breastfeeding... open atmosphere with friendly service... tables are well spaced so you don't feel like your kid is annoying the diners nearby (it's usually full of kids anyway)..."

Children's menu	✓	$$	Prices
Changing station	✓	❹	Customer service
Highchairs/boosters	✓	❹	Stroller access

WWW.CPK.COM

BALTIMORE—201 E PRATT ST (AT HARBORPLACE); 410.783.9339; M-TH 11:30-10, F-SA 11:30-11, SU 12-9 ; MALL PARKING

Cheesecake Factory, The

"...although their cheesecake is good, we come here for the kid-friendly atmosphere and selection of good food... eclectic menu has something for everyone... they will bring your tot a plate of yogurt, cheese, bananas and bread free of charge... we love how flexible they are—they'll make whatever my kids want... lots of mommies here... always fun and always crazy... no real kids menu, but the pizza is great to share... waits can be really long..."

Children's menu	×	$$$	Prices
Changing station	✓	❹	Customer service
Highchairs/boosters	✓	❸	Stroller access

WWW.THECHEESECAKEFACTORY.COM/

BALTIMORE—201 E PRATT ST (AT S CALVERT ST); 410.234.3990; M-TH 11:30-11, F-SA 11:30-12:30, SU 10-10

Chicken Out

"...great place for a quick family friendly bite .. pulled chicken kid's meal is a hit with my little one... this is a great place to go for an upscale homemade meal... uses fresh ingredients and has wonderful side dishes to choose from .. don't forget to leave room for the many layered chocolate cake or the sumptuous (also several layers) carrot cake..."

Children's menu	×	$$	Prices
Changing station	×	❸	Customer service
Highchairs/boosters	×	❹	Stroller access

WWW.CHICKENOUT.COM

BALTIMORE—1809 REISTERSTOWN RD (OFF RT 695); 410.484.5401; M-SA 11-9, SU 11-8:30

Chili's Grill & Bar

"...family-friendly, mild Mexican fare... delicious ribs, soups, salads... kids' menu and crayons as you sit down... on the noisy side, so you don't mind if your kids talk in their usual loud voices... service is excellent... fun night out with the family... a wide variety of menu selections for kids and their parents—all at a reasonable price... best chicken fingers on any kids' menu..."

Children's menu	✓	$$	Prices
Changing station	✓	❹	Customer service
Highchairs/boosters	✓	❹	Stroller access

WWW.CHILIS.COM

BALTIMORE—8119 HONEYGO BLVD (AT WHITE MARSH MALL); 410.933.0089; SU-TH 11-11, F-SA 11-12AM

Chipotle Mexican Grill

"...higher-end burritos and tacos... I don't think I've ever been in one when there weren't kids running around... given that the burritos are enormous, I usually just get one and share it with my two boys... plenty of room for strollers and plenty of noise for screaming babies... fresh and tasty..."

Children's menu .... ✗ | $ .... Prices
Changing station .... ✗ | ❹ .... Customer service
Highchairs/boosters .... ✓ | ❹ .... Stroller access

WWW.CHIPOTLE.COM

BALTIMORE—621 E PRATT ST (AT MARKET PL); 410.837.8353; DAILY 11-10; FREE PARKING

BALTIMORE—6314 YORK RD (AT RT 45); 410.377.7728; M-SA 10-11; FREE PARKING

Cici's Pizza

"...a great buffet for easy dining with kids... pizza at the right price... kids 3 and under eat free... very crowded during lunch and dinner rushes... not much room for strollers, but they'll help you find a place to stash it... they always have birthday parties and it's usually very crowded and noisy... pizza, pasta and salad buffet for under $10..."

Children's menu .... ✓ | $ .... Prices
Changing station .... ✓ | ❹ .... Customer service
Highchairs/boosters .... ✓ | ❹ .... Stroller access

WWW.CICISPIZZA.COM

BALTIMORE—6473 BALTIMORE NATIONAL PIKE (OFF ROLLING RD); 410.719.1001; SU-TH 11-10, F-SA 11-11; PARKING IN FRONT OF BLDG

Egyptian Pizza

"...great pizza... only place I've found that offers a soy cheese pizza, for those of us that are lactose intolerant... the staff is extremely family friendly and accommodating... we took our daughter there several times before she began walking..."

Children's menu .... ✓ | $$ .... Prices
Changing station .... ✗ | ❺ .... Customer service
Highchairs/boosters .... ✓ | ❹ .... Stroller access

WWW.EGYPTIANPIZZA.COM

BALTIMORE—542 E BELVEDERE AVE (AT HWY 45); 410.323.7060; DAILY 11-11

ESPN Zone

"...loud and crazy with average food... kids like to play the arcade games and carry the beeper, which alerts diners when their table is ready... we avoid it during big sporting events... lots of room for strollers... staff is friendly and accommodating..."

Children's menu .... ✓ | $$$ .... Prices
Changing station .... ✓ | ❹ .... Customer service
Highchairs/boosters .... ✓ | ❸ .... Stroller access

WWW.ESPNZONE.COM

BALTIMORE—601 E PRATT ST (OFF S PRESIDENT ST); 410.685.3776; SU-TH 11-12, SA 11-1

Friendly's

"...we love Friendly's because it's fast, fun and the food is pretty good... you may wait a bit for your service, but given the promise of a sundae most kids will persevere... colorful menu and M&M pancakes... desert and a drink are included with some kids meals... convenient if you have kids of varying ages—there's something good for everyone... burgers, sandwiches and more fries than you'll know what to do with..."

Children's menu .... ✓ $$ .... Prices
Changing station.......................... ✓ ❸ .... Customer service
Highchairs/boosters .... ✓ ❸ ....Stroller access

WWW.FRIENDLYS.COM

BALTIMORE—8200 PERRY HALL BLVD (AT WHITE MARSH MALL); 410.931.7216; SU-TH 7-11, F-SA 7-12

BALTIMORE—9551 BEL AIR RD (AT CHAPEL RD); 410.256.2120; SU-TH 7-11, F-SA 7-12

Fuddruckers

“...a super burger chain with fresh and tasty food... colorful and noisy with lots of distraction until the food arrives... loads of fresh toppings so that you can make your perfectly cooked burger even better... great kids deals that come with a free treat... noise not a problem in this super casual atmosphere... some locations have video games in the back which will buy you an extra half hour if you need it... low-key and very family friendly...”

Children's menu .... ✓ $$ .... Prices
Changing station.......................... ✓ ❹ .... Customer service
Highchairs/boosters .... ✓ ❹ ....Stroller access

WWW.FUDDRUCKERS.COM

BALTIMORE—125 MARKET PL (AT E LOMBARD ST); 410.625.0995; DAILY 11-9; FREE PARKING

BALTIMORE—8200 PERRY HALL BLVD (AT WHITE MARSH MALL); 410.933.3884; DAILY 11-9

Gertrudes

“...wonderful restaurant by legend, it is a fabulous place to go to for brunch (or any other time for the matter). there are crab omelettes and stuffed French toast to choose from .. specialize in an assortment of fresh seafood dishes... in the warm weather, it is nice to sit out in the gardens by the flowers and fountains... a good dinner stop after a day at the BMA...”

Children's menu .... ✗ $$$ .... Prices
Changing station.......................... ✗ ❺ .... Customer service
Highchairs/boosters .... ✓ ❸ ....Stroller access

WWW.GERTRUDESBALTIMORE.COM

BALTIMORE—10 ART MUSEUM DR (OFF 29TH ST); 410.889.3399; T-F 11:30AM-9PM SA 10:30AM-9PM SU DAILY 10:30-8

Golden West Cafe

“...this is our standard for family friendly dining... food is great and the atmosphere is relatively welcoming for kids... they even have a few toys...”

Children's menu .... ✓ $ .... Prices
Changing station.......................... ✓ ❹ .... Customer service
Highchairs/boosters .... ✓ ❺ ....Stroller access

BALTIMORE—1105 W 36TH ST (AT HICKORY AVE); 410.889.8891; M W-SU 9-10

Hard Rock Cafe

“...fun and tasty if you can get in... the lines can be horrendous so be sure to check in with them first... a good spot if you have tots in tow—food tastes good and the staff is clearly used to messy eaters... hectic and loud... fun for adults as well as kids...”

Children's menu .... ✓ $$$ .... Prices
Changing station.......................... ✓ ❹ .... Customer service
Highchairs/boosters .... ✓ ❸ ....Stroller access

WWW.HARDROCK.COM

BALTIMORE—601 E PRATT ST (AT GAY ST); 410.347.7625; SU-TH 11-12AM, F-SA 11-2AM

IKEA

"...Swedish meatballs and funny berry drinks—all yummy and cheap... a clean, comfortable place to eat... the restaurant sells baby food and has bottle/jar warmers... worth visiting even if you aren't shopping—the food is cheap, but good... totally kid-friendly... lines can sometimes be long, especially during peak shopping hours..."

Children's menu ✓ | $$ Prices
Changing station ✓ | ❹ Customer service
Highchairs/boosters ✓ | ❹ Stroller access

WWW.IKEA.COM

BALTIMORE—8352 HONEYGO BLVD (AT WHITE MARSH MALL); 410.931.5400; M-F 10-9, SA 9-9, SU 10-8

Maria D's

"...want to grab a quick lunch while you're in Federal Hill... get a slice of pizza at Maria D's... good thin-crust pizza... no highchairs, but there's room for the stroller in the restaurant..."

Children's menu ✓ | $ Prices
Changing station × | ❸ Customer service
Highchairs/boosters ✓ | ❺ Stroller access

BALTIMORE—1016 LIGHT ST (AT POULTNEY ST); 410.727.5430; M-TH 11-2, F-SA 11-2:30

McCormick & Schmicks

"...steak and seafood are the mainstay but the menu is broad... terrific happy-hour menu... a little more formal than your regular 'tot-friendly' restaurant, but the staff is great and goes out of their way to make sure you're comfortable... try to get one of the banquet rooms—it makes breastfeeding much easier... good food for adults and more than enough for the little ones too..."

Children's menu ✓ | $$$ Prices
Changing station ✓ | ❹ Customer service
Highchairs/boosters ✓ | ❹ Stroller access

WWW.MCCORMICKANDSCHMICKS.COM

BALTIMORE—711 EASTERN AVE (AT PRESIDENT ST); 410.234.1300; SU-TH 11:30-11, F-SA 11:30-12

Mount Vernon Stable And Saloon

"...go early... had a great time and the service was very nice—they had balloons waiting at the table as we'd reserved ahead... don't miss the peanut butter pie..."

Children's menu × | $$$ Prices
Changing station × | ❺ Customer service
Highchairs/boosters ✓ | ❷ Stroller access

WWW.MVSTABLE.COM

BALTIMORE—909 N CHARLES ST (AT READ ST); 410.685.7427; SU-TH 10-12, F-SA 10-1

Olive Garden

"...finally a place that is both kid and adult friendly... tasty Italian chain with lot's of convenient locations... the staff consistently attends to the details of dining with babies and toddlers—minimizing wait time, highchairs offered spontaneously, bread sticks brought immediately... food is served as quickly as possible... happy to create special orders... our waitress even acted as our family photographer..."

Children's menu ✓ | $$ Prices
Changing station ✓ | ❹ Customer service
Highchairs/boosters ✓ | ❹ Stroller access

WWW.OLIVEGARDEN.COM

BALTIMORE—8245 PERRY HALL BLVD (AT HONEYGO BLVD); 410.931.3316; SU-TH 11-10, F-SA 11-11

One World Cafe

"...good option for food that is healthy and tasty... have always been accommodating by making our kids things that aren't on the menu... have highchairs, but not many... they consistently have good brunch choices... definitely try the special of the day... it's a vegetarian mom's dream come true..."

Children's menu .... × $$$ .... Prices
Changing station .... ×   ❹ .... Customer service
Highchairs/boosters .... ✓   ❸ .... Stroller access

WWW.ONE-WORLD-CAFE.COM

BALTIMORE—100 W UNIVERSITY PKWY (OFF 40TH ST); 410.235.5777; M-SA 7:30-2, SU 8-5

Panera Bread

"...soups, sandwiches and delicious desserts... self-service food at great prices... the booths are big enough to put your car seat and store your stuff... fresh bread make their sandwiches special... some locations have a have a community room which is a great place for my moms group to sit, park our strollers and breast feed if need be..."

Children's menu .... × $$ .... Prices
Changing station .... ✓   ❹ .... Customer service
Highchairs/boosters .... ✓   ❹ .... Stroller access

WWW.PANERABREAD.COM

BALTIMORE—6307 YORK RD (AT WALKER AVE); 410.433.9174; M-SA 6-9, SU 6-8

Red Canoe

"...a cozy bookstore cafe that offers coffee, pastries and light meals... kids like the soda type drinks... super family friendly, they even host writing classes and hikes..."

Children's menu .... × $$$ .... Prices
Changing station .... ×   ❸ .... Customer service
Highchairs/boosters .... ×   ❸ .... Stroller access

WWW.REDCANOE.BZ

BALTIMORE—4337 HARFORD RD (AT COLD SPRING LN); 410.444.4440; M-T 7:30-2, W-SA 7:30-5, SU 10-3; FREE PARKING

Rocky Run Tap & Grill

Children's menu .... ✓   × .... Changing station
Highchairs/boosters .... ✓

WWW.ROCKYRUN.COM

BALTIMORE—3105 ST PAUL ST (OFF 33RD ST); 410.235.2501; M-TH 11-1, F-SA 11-2, SU 11-12 AM

Yabba Pot

"...a vegetarian restaurant in Baltimore... the best bet for a cheap, hot vegetarian meal in Charles Village... use mostly locally grown produce as well as organic products as much as they can..."

Children's menu .... × $$$ .... Prices
Changing station .... ✓   ❸ .... Customer service
Highchairs/boosters .... ✓   ❸ .... Stroller access

BALTIMORE—2433 ST PAUL ST (OFF 25TH ST); 410.662.8638; M-F 11:30-8, SA 11:30-9; PARKING LOT

North of Baltimore

"lila picks"

★Panera Bread

★Romano's Macaroni Grill

Baja Fresh

"...Mexican food using all fresh ingredients... many restaurants have a nice outdoor courtyard—which is good if you are self-conscious about a loud baby... casual atmosphere... my son loves the fresh salsa... I was able to keep the stroller next to me throughout my meal... I was able to get milk and juice for my kid's meal..."

Children's menu ✓ | $$ Prices
Changing station ✗ | ❹ Customer service
Highchairs/boosters ✓ | ❸ Stroller access

WWW.BAJAFRESH.COM

LUTHERVILLE—2080 YORK RD (AT TIMONIUM RD); 410.561.1050; M-TH 11-9, F-SA 11-10

Bertucci's Brick Oven Pizzeria

"...a laid back Italian eatery with delicious Italian grub... pizza, pasta, something for everyone... get the olive oil for dipping, this makes waiting for the pizza a bearable experience with hungry tots... not an obviously kid-friendly restaurant, but they do a good job of accommodating parents with tots... great kids menu... it can get busy, so go early... finding room for strollers can be challenging, but the staff is very accommodating..."

Children's menu ✓ | $$ Prices
Changing station ✓ | ❹ Customer service
Highchairs/boosters ✓ | ❹ Stroller access

WWW.BERTUCCIS.COM

BEL AIR—12 BEL AIR S PKWY (AT RT 24); 410.569.4600; M-SA 11-10; FREE PARKING

Bill Bateman's Bistro

"...great food and great service... well done kids menu, fitting the well done lively and active bistro... don't worry about making a ruckus, or a mess here... staff is great and happily accommodates families with little children..."

Children's menu ✗ | $$ Prices
Changing station ✗ | ❹ Customer service
Highchairs/boosters ✓ | ❹ Stroller access

WWW.BILLBATEMAN.COM

TOWSON—7800 YORK RD (AT RT 45); 410.296.2737; DAILY 11-1; FREE PARKING

Bob Evans Farms Restaurant ★★★★☆

"...home style cooking... worth the wait for their breakfast... arrive early to beat the weekend crowds... slings available for car seats... kid-friendly... reasonable prices... sausage, eggs and hot cakes... easy food—especially if you have picky eaters with you..."

Children's menu	✓	$$	Prices
Changing station	✓	❹	Customer service
Highchairs/boosters	✓	❹	Stroller access

WWW.BOBEVANS.COM

TIMONIUM—400 W PADONIA RD (AT DEERECO RD); 410.308.3740; SU 7-9, M-TH 6-9, F-SA 7-6

TOWSON—8607 LASALLE RD (AT PUTTY HILL AVE); 410.494.0384; DAILY 6-10

Cheeburger Cheeburger

"...old time feel... classic 50's and 60's rock and roll on the radio... big, big burgers—salads too... you can choose whatever topping you want for your burgers and salads... great shakes... don't miss the clown on Friday nights—free face painting and my kids love it... good food and a very relaxed environment..."

Children's menu	✓	$$	Prices
Changing station	✓	❹	Customer service
Highchairs/boosters	✓	❸	Stroller access

WWW.CHEEBURGER.COM

BEL AIR—5 BEL AIR S PKWY (AT HWY 924); 410.569.7774; M-SA 11-9; FREE PARKING

TIMONIUM—2135 E YORK RD (AT TIMONIUM RD); 410.252.4466; M-SA 11-9

Chili's Grill & Bar

"...family-friendly, mild Mexican fare... delicious ribs, soups, salads... kids' menu and crayons as you sit down... on the noisy side, so you don't mind if your kids talk in their usual loud voices... service is excellent... fun night out with the family... a wide variety of menu selections for kids and their parents—all at a reasonable price... best chicken fingers on any kids' menu..."

Children's menu	✓	$$	Prices
Changing station	✓	❹	Customer service
Highchairs/boosters	✓	❹	Stroller access

WWW.CHILIS.COM

BEL AIR—502 BALTIMORE PIK (AT VIETNAM VETS MEM HWY); 410.638.2992; SU-TH 11-11, F-SA 11-12

TIMONIUM—9615 DEERECO RD (OFF RT 83); 410.308.8740; SU-TH 11-11, F-SA 11-12

Chipotle Mexican Grill

"...higher-end burritos and tacos... I don't think I've ever been in one when there weren't kids running around... given that the burritos are enormous, I usually just get one and share it with my two boys... plenty of room for strollers and plenty of noise for screaming babies... fresh and tasty..."

Children's menu	×	$	Prices
Changing station	×	❹	Customer service
Highchairs/boosters	✓	❹	Stroller access

WWW.CHIPOTLE.COM

BEL AIR—5 BEL AIR S PKY (AT HWY 924); 410.515.0547; DAILY 11-10

HUNT VALLEY—112 SHAWAN RD (AT HUNT VALLEY MALL); 410.771.6025; M-SA 10-11; FREE PARKING

Friendly's

"...we love Friendly's because it's fast, fun and the food is pretty good... you may wait a bit for your service, but given the promise of a sundae most kids will persevere... colorful menu and M&M pancakes... desert and a drink are included with some kids meals... convenient if you have kids of varying ages—there's something good for everyone... burgers, sandwiches and more fries than you'll know what to do with..."

Children's menu ✓ | $$ Prices
Changing station ✓ | ❸ Customer service
Highchairs/boosters ✓ | ❸ Stroller access

WWW.FRIENDLYS.COM

BEL AIR—353 S MAIN ST (AT BAILEYS LN); 410.838.7374; DAILY 11-9; FREE PARKING

BEL AIR—600 BALTIMORE PIKE (AT HARFORD MALL); 410.838.8565; DAILY 11-9; FREE PARKING

LUTHERVILLE—1414 YORK RD (AT WESTBURY RD); 410.823.4723; DAILY 11-9; FREE PARKING

Moe's Southwest Grill

"...fresh Mex food—burritos, quesedillas and tacos... there always are a ton of babies and kids there... if you want a drink other than juice or soda, bring your own sippy cup... tasty, good quality, cheap chow that satisfies both young and old... kids' meals for less than $3 and free on Monday nights... they only serve sodas and fruit punch for the kids..."

Children's menu ✓ | $$ Prices
Changing station ✓ | ❹ Customer service
Highchairs/boosters ✓ | ❹ Stroller access

WWW.MOES.COM

COCKEYSVILLE—10015 YORK RD (AT CRANBROOK RD); 410.667.6637; DAILY 11-10

Nautilus Diner

"...this is a great diner that has a great selection and really caters to kids .. omelets and Belgian waffles (with or without fruit)are superb... portions for the Greek specialties are quite generous..."

Children's menu ✓ | $$$ Prices
Changing station × | ❺ Customer service
Highchairs/boosters ✓ | ❸ Stroller access

TIMONIUM—2047 YORK RD (OFF TIMONIUM RD); 410.561.8826; OPEN 24 HRS

Panera Bread

"...soups, sandwiches and delicious desserts... self-service food at great prices... the booths are big enough to put your car seat and store your stuff... fresh bread make their sandwiches special... some locations have a have a community room which is a great place for my moms group to sit, park our strollers and breast feed if need be..."

Children's menu × | $$ Prices
Changing station ✓ | ❹ Customer service
Highchairs/boosters ✓ | ❹ Stroller access

WWW.PANERABREAD.COM

TIMONIUM—2131 YORK RD (AT E TIMONIUM RD); 410.453.9840; M-SA 6-9, SU 7-8

TOWSON—1238 PUTTY HILL AVE (AT GOUCHER BLVD); 410.821.9111; M-SA 6-9, SU 7-8

Red Robin

"...very kid-oriented—loud, balloons, bright lights, colorful decor and a cheerful staff make Red Robin a favorite among parents and children... the food is mainly burgers (beef or chicken)... loud music

covers even the most boisterous of screaming... lots of kids—all the time... sometimes the wait can be long, but the arcade games and balloons help pass the time... ”

Children's menu ✓	$$ Prices
Changing station ✓	❹ Customer service
Highchairs/boosters ✓	❹ Stroller access

WWW.REDROBIN.COM

TOWSON—1238 PUTTY HILL AVE (AT GOUCHER BLVD); 410.823.4224; SU-TH 11-10, F-SA 11-11

Romano's Macaroni Grill

“*...family oriented and tasty... noisy so nobody cares if your kids make noise... the staff goes out of their way to make families feel welcome... they even provide slings by the table for infant carriers... the noise level is pretty constant so it's not too loud, but loud enough so that crying babies don't disturb the other patrons... good kids' menu with somewhat healthy items... crayons for kids to color on the paper tablecloths...* ”

Children's menu ✓	$$$ Prices
Changing station ✓	❹ Customer service
Highchairs/boosters ✓	❹ Stroller access

WWW.MACARONIGRILL.COM

TIMONIUM—9701 BEAVER DAM RD (OFF DEERECO RD); 410.628.7112; SU-TH 11-10, F-SA 11-11

Ruby Tuesday

“*...nice variety of healthy choices on the kids' menu—turkey, spaghetti, chicken tenders... you can definitely find something healthy here... prices are on the high side, but at least everyone can find something they like... service is fast and efficient... my daughter makes a mess and they never let me clean it up... your typical chain, but it works—you'll be happy to see ample aisle space, storage for your stroller, and attentive staff...* ”

Children's menu ✓	$$ Prices
Changing station ✓	❹ Customer service
Highchairs/boosters ✓	❸ Stroller access

WWW.RUBYTUESDAY.COM

BEL AIR—593 BALTIMORE PIKE (AT HARFORD MALL); 410.638.0903; M-TH 11-11, F-SA 11-12, SU 11-10

Strapazza

“*...wonderful Italian cuisine in clean, well-designed spaces... healthy pasta, salads and other Italian dishes... they provided us with highchairs and were very accommodating with our tots... atmosphere is quiet and peaceful...* ”

Children's menu ✓	$$$ Prices
Changing station ✗	❹ Customer service
Highchairs/boosters ✓	❸ Stroller access

WWW.STRAPAZZA.COM

TOWSON—12 W ALLEGHANY AVE (AT YORK RD); 410.296.5577; SU-TH 10-10, F-SA 10-11; PARKING IN FRONT OF BLDG

TGI Friday's

“*...good old American bar food with a reasonable selection for the healthier set as well... I love that the kids meal includes salad... my daughter requests the potato skins on a regular basis (which is good because they are also my favorite)... moderately priced... cheerful servers are used to the mess my kids leave behind... relaxed scene... I'd steer clear on a Friday night unless you don't mind waiting and watching the singles scene...* ”

Children's menu ✓	$$ Prices

Changing station .... ✓ ❹ .... Customer service
Highchairs/boosters .... ✓ ❸ .... Stroller access

WWW.TGIFRIDAYS.COM

BEL AIR—615 BEL AIR PIKE BLDG E UNIT Z (AT HARFORD MALL); 410.420.6766; DAILY 11:30-1:30

TOWSON—825 DULANEY VALLEY RD (AT TOWSON TOWN CTR); 410.828.4556; DAILY 11-2

West of Baltimore

"lila picks"

★New Towne Diner

★Panera Bread

Bill Bateman's Bistro

"...great food and great service... well done kids menu, fitting the well done lively and active bistro... don't worry about making a ruckus, or a mess here... staff is great and happily accommodates families with little children..."

Children's menu	×	$$	Prices
Changing station	×	4	Customer service
Highchairs/boosters	✓	4	Stroller access

WWW.BILLBATEMAN.COM

REISTERSTOWN—102 CHARTLEY DR (AT RT 140); 410.526.6200; DAILY 11-1; FREE PARKING

Bob Evans Farms Restaurant

"...home style cooking... worth the wait for their breakfast... arrive early to beat the weekend crowds... slings available for car seats... kid-friendly... reasonable prices... sausage, eggs and hot cakes... easy food—especially if you have picky eaters with you..."

Children's menu	✓	$$	Prices
Changing station	✓	4	Customer service
Highchairs/boosters	✓	4	Stroller access

WWW.BOBEVANS.COM

CATONSVILLE—6336 BALTIMORE NATIONAL PIKE (AT ROLLING RD); 410.744.1010; DAILY 6-10

Bombay Peacock Grill

"...family friendly and has a great lunch and weekend buffet with lots of things to choose from... they also have some items on the menu for kids to eat that are more in the 'kid-friendly' taste arena..."

Children's menu	×	$$$	Prices
Changing station	×	4	Customer service
Highchairs/boosters	✓	4	Stroller access

WWW.BOMBAYGRILL.COM

OWINGS MILLS—11308 REISTERSTOWN RD (AT RT 140); 410.998.9295; SU-TH 11:30-10, F-SA 11:30-11

Cheeburger Cheeburger

"...old time feel... classic 50's and 60's rock and roll on the radio... big, big burgers—salads too... you can choose whatever topping you want for your burgers and salads... great shakes... don't miss the clown on Friday nights—free face painting and my kids love it... good food and a very relaxed environment..."

Children's menu	✓	$$	Prices

Changing station .... ✓ ❹ .... Customer service
Highchairs/boosters .... ✓ ❸ .... Stroller access

WWW.CHEEBURGER.COM

OWINGS MILLS—10995 OWINGS MILLS BLVD (AT RT 140); 410.363.3007; SU-TH 11-9, F-SA 11-10

Dairy Fresh ★★★★★

"...this family owned place is the best place around to go for homemade custard and Italian ice .. great prices and many sizes to choose from; you can even mix flavors... the selections for the Italian ice change daily and are always fresh... the custard is made from fresh milk that is brought in twice a week straight from the farm..."

Children's menu .... ✗ $ .... Prices
Changing station .... ✗ ❺ .... Customer service
Highchairs/boosters .... ✗ ❺ .... Stroller access

REISTERSTOWN—201 MAIN ST (AT COCKEYS MILL RD); 410.526.1800; M-TH 11-10, F-SA 11-11

Don Pablo's ★★★★☆

"...yummy Mexican dishes... spacious and super kid-friendly—we've been coming here since our baby was 2 weeks old... kid's meals are inexpensive and plentiful... my son loves playing with the dough and the meal arrives in no time... fun, boisterous setting... can get busy, but you generally get a table with little delay..."

Children's menu .... ✓ $$ .... Prices
Changing station .... ✓ ❹ .... Customer service
Highchairs/boosters .... ✓ ❹ .... Stroller access

WWW.DONPABLOS.COM

OWINGS MILLS—ONE RESTAURANT PARK DR (OFF PAINTERS MILL RD); 410.902.0300; SU-TH 11:30-10, F-SA 11:30-11

Friendly's ★★★½☆

"...we love Friendly's because it's fast, fun and the food is pretty good... you may wait a bit for your service, but given the promise of a sundae most kids will persevere... colorful menu and M&M pancakes... desert and a drink are included with some kids meals... convenient if you have kids of varying ages—there's something good for everyone... burgers, sandwiches and more fries than you'll know what to do with..."

Children's menu .... ✓ $$ .... Prices
Changing station .... ✓ ❸ .... Customer service
Highchairs/boosters .... ✓ ❸ .... Stroller access

WWW.FRIENDLYS.COM

CATONSVILLE—748 FREDERICK RD (AT BLOOMSBURY AVE); 410.869.3620; DAILY 11-9; FREE PARKING

REISTERSTOWN—75 MAIN ST (AT E CHATSWORTH AVE); 410.517.1163; DAILY 11-9; FREE PARKING

Fuddruckers ★★★★☆

"...a super burger chain with fresh and tasty food... colorful and noisy with lots of distraction until the food arrives... loads of fresh toppings so that you can make your perfectly cooked burger even better... great kids deals that come with a free treat... noise not a problem in this super casual atmosphere... some locations have video games in the back which will buy you an extra half hour if you need it... low-key and very family friendly..."

Children's menu .... ✓ $$ .... Prices
Changing station .... ✓ ❹ .... Customer service
Highchairs/boosters .... ✓ ❹ .... Stroller access

WWW.FUDDRUCKERS.COM

OWINGS MILLS—11515 REISTERSTOWN RD (AT SUNSET RD); 410.654.3001; DAILY 11-9; FREE PARKING

PIKESVILLE—1700 REISTERSTOWN RD (AT VILLAGE RD); 410.653.7750; DAILY 11-9; FREE PARKING

Java Mammas

"...great place to go and sip a cup of coffee in the historical 'antique row' part of Reisterstown... fun atmosphere and yet feels relaxing... very family friendly, they have toys and games for kids... there's a room I the back with big comty chairs that's good to hang out with other moms and babies in..."

Children's menu .... ✗ | $$ .... Prices
Changing station .... ✓ | ❹ .... Customer service
Highchairs/boosters .... ✓ | ❸ .... Stroller access

WWW.JAVAMAMMAS.COM

REISTERSTOWN—324 MAIN ST (AT GOLDSBOROUGH WAY); 410.833.8100; SU-TH 6-9:30, F-SA 7-11

New Towne Diner

"...great place that has everything for everybody with very reasonable prices... the food is quick and there is never a long wait to eat... food is okay, but it's the busy atmosphere that really makes it kid-friendly... breakfast is best here..."

Children's menu .... ✓ | $$ .... Prices
Changing station .... ✗ | ❸ .... Customer service
Highchairs/boosters .... ✓ | ❸ .... Stroller access

OWINGS MILLS—11316 REISTERSTOWN RD (AT RT 140); 410.654.0066; SU-TH 7-12, F-SA 7-1

Panera Bread

"...soups, sandwiches and delicious desserts... self-service food at great prices... the booths are big enough to put your car seat and store your stuff... fresh bread make their sandwiches special... some locations have a have a community room which is a great place for my moms group to sit, park our strollers and breast feed if need be..."

Children's menu .... ✗ | $$ .... Prices
Changing station .... ✓ | ❹ .... Customer service
Highchairs/boosters .... ✓ | ❹ .... Stroller access

WWW.PANERABREAD.COM

OWINGS MILLS—1852 REISTERTOWN RD (OFF I-695); 410.602.5125; M-SA 6-9, SU 7-8

Red Robin

"...very kid-oriented—loud, balloons, bright lights, colorful decor and a cheerful staff make Red Robin a favorite among parents and children... the food is mainly burgers (beef or chicken)... loud music covers even the most boisterous of screaming... lots of kids—all the time... sometimes the wait can be long, but the arcade games and balloons help pass the time..."

Children's menu .... ✓ | $$ .... Prices
Changing station .... ✓ | ❹ .... Customer service
Highchairs/boosters .... ✓ | ❹ .... Stroller access

WWW.REDROBIN.COM

OWINGS MILLS—4 RESTAURANT PARK DR (AT OWINGS MILLS BLVD); 443.394.0999; SU-TH 11-10, F-SA 11-11

Strapazza

"...wonderful Italian cuisine in clean, well-designed spaces... healthy pasta, salads and other Italian dishes... they provided us with highchairs and were very accomodating with our tots... atmosphere is quiet and peaceful..."

Children's menu ✓ | $$$ Prices
Changing station ✗ | ❹ Customer service
Highchairs/boosters ✓ | ❸ Stroller access

WWW.STRAPAZZA.COM

PIKESVILLE—1330 REISTERSTOWN RD (OFF SUDBROOK LN); 410.484.6906; SU-TH 10-10, F-SA 10-11; PARKING IN FRONT OF BLDG

Suburban House Restaurant ★★★☆☆

"...decor is a little out dated but the food is superb and prices even better... a rarity for a restaurant in the area to have its own parking lot... an okay spot for lunch, but gets crowded at dinnertime... good service..."

Children's menu ✗ | $ Prices
Changing station ✗ | ❹ Customer service
Highchairs/boosters ✓ | ❷ Stroller access

WWW.SUBURBANHOUSEDELI.COM

PIKESVILLE—911 REISTERSTOWN RD (AT HAWTHORNE AVE); 410.484.7775; DAILY 7-10

TGI Friday's ★★★★☆

"...good old American bar food with a reasonable selection for the healthier set as well... I love that the kids meal includes salad... my daughter requests the potato skins on a regular basis (which is good because they are also my favorite)... moderately priced... cheerful servers are used to the mess my kids leave behind... relaxed scene... I'd steer clear on a Friday night unless you don't mind waiting and watching the singles scene..."

Children's menu ✓ | $$ Prices
Changing station ✓ | ❹ Customer service
Highchairs/boosters ✓ | ❸ Stroller access

WWW.TGIFRIDAYS.COM

OWINGS MILLS—9634 REISTERSTOWN RD (AT RT 140); 410.363.8116; DAILY 11-12:45; PARKING LOT

The Backfin Seafood & Family Restaurant ★☆☆☆☆

"...this is the place to go for crabcakes and crab soup... kids always welcome..."

Children's menu ✗ | $$$ Prices
Changing station ✗ | ❸ Customer service
Highchairs/boosters ✓ | ❸ Stroller access

PIKESVILLE—1116 REISTERSTOWN RD (AT SUDBROOK LN); 410.484.7344; T-SA 11-10, SU 1-9; PARKING LOT

South of Baltimore

"lila picks"

★Chevy's Fresh Mex
★Duclaw Brewing Co
★Johnny Rockets
★Romano's Macaroni Grill
★Texas Roadhouse

restaurants

Bertucci's Brick Oven Pizzeria

"...a laid back Italian eatery with delicious Italian grub... pizza, pasta, something for everyone... get the olive oil for dipping, this makes waiting for the pizza a bearable experience with hungry tots... not an obviously kid-friendly restaurant, but they do a good job of accommodating parents with tots... great kids menu... it can get busy, so go early... finding room for strollers can be challenging, but the staff is very accommodating..."

Children's menu .... ✓ | $$ .... Prices
Changing station.......................... ✓ | ❹ .... Customer service
Highchairs/boosters .... ✓ | ❹ .... Stroller access

WWW.BERTUCCIS.COM

ANNAPOLIS—2207 FORREST DR (OFF WEST ST); 410.266.5800; M-TH 11-10, F-SA 11-11, SU 12-10; FREE PARKING

Bill Bateman's Bistro

"...great food and great service... well done kids menu, fitting the well done lively and active bistro... don't worry about making a ruckus, or a mess here... staff is great and happily accommodates families with little children..."

Children's menu .... × | $$ .... Prices
Changing station.......................... × | ❹ .... Customer service
Highchairs/boosters .... ✓ | ❹ .... Stroller access

WWW.BILLBATEMAN.COM

SEVERNA PARK—566 GOV RITCHIE HWY (AT MCKINSEY RD); 410.315.7060, SU-TH 11-12 ,F-SA 11-1

California Pizza Kitchen

"...you can't go wrong with their fabulous pizza... always clean... the food's great, the kids drinks all come with a lid... the staff is super friendly to kids... crayons and coloring books keep little minds busy... most locations have a place for strollers at the front... no funny looks or attitude when breastfeeding... open atmosphere with friendly service... tables are well spaced so you don't feel like your kid is annoying the diners nearby (it's usually full of kids anyway)..."

Children's menu .... ✓ | $$ .... Prices
Changing station.......................... ✓ | ❹ .... Customer service
Highchairs/boosters .... ✓ | ❹ .... Stroller access

WWW.CPK.COM

ANNAPOLIS—1870 ANNAPOLIS MALL (AT ANNAPOLIS MALL); 410.573.2060; M-TH 11:30-10, F-SA 11:30-11, SU 12-9 ; MALL PARKING

Cheeburger Cheeburger

"...old time feel... classic 50's and 60's rock and roll on the radio... big, big burgers—salads too... you can choose whatever topping you want for your burgers and salads... great shakes... don't miss the clown on Friday nights—free face painting and my kids love it... good food and a very relaxed environment..."

Children's menu.......................... ✓ $$.. Prices
Changing station .... ✓ ❹ ....Customer service
Highchairs/boosters..................... ✓ ❸ .... Stroller access

WWW.CHEEBURGER.COM

ANNAPOLIS—2329 B FOREST DR (AT RT 2); 410.224.7297; SU-TH 11-9, F-SA 11-10; FREE PARKING

Chevys Fresh Mex

"...a nice combo of good food for adults and a nice kid's menu... always a sure bet with tots in tow... tasty Mexican food with a simple kids menu (especially the quesedillas)... the tortilla making machine is sure to grab your toddler's attention until the food arrives... an occasional balloon making man... party-like atmosphere with colorful decorations... huge Margaritas for mom and dad... service generally excellent and fast, but you may have to wait for a table at peak hours... long tables can accommodate the multifamily get-together..."

Children's menu.......................... ✓ $$.. Prices
Changing station .... ✓ ❹ ....Customer service
Highchairs/boosters..................... ✓ ❹ .... Stroller access

WWW.CHEVYS.COM

ANNAPOLIS—2430 SOLOMONS ISLAND RD (AT HIGHWAY 2); 410.573.4939; SU-TH 11-10, F-SA 11-11; STREET PARKING

HANOVER—7000 ARUNDEL MILLS CIR (AT ARUNDEL MILLS MALL); 410.799.1505; SU-TH 11-10, F-SA 11-11; MALL PARKING

Chili's Grill & Bar

"...family-friendly, mild Mexican fare... delicious ribs, soups, salads... kids' menu and crayons as you sit down... on the noisy side, so you don't mind if your kids talk in their usual loud voices... service is excellent... fun night out with the family... a wide variety of menu selections for kids and their parents—all at a reasonable price... best chicken fingers on any kids' menu..."

Children's menu.......................... ✓ $$.. Prices
Changing station .... ✓ ❹ ....Customer service
Highchairs/boosters..................... ✓ ❹ .... Stroller access

WWW.CHILIS.COM

ANNAPOLIS—2339 FOREST DR (AT RIVA RD); 410.266.9737; SU-TH 11-10, F-SA 11-11; FREE PARKING

HANOVER—7000 ARUNDEL MILLS CIR (AT ARUNDEL MILLS MALL); 410.796.0200; SU-TH 11-11, F-SA 11-12AM

Duclaw Brewing Co

"...nice kid's menu, family friendly restaurant... staff is very patient and attentive with children... we have found them to be the most accommodating... they also bring the kids food as quick as possible and you don't have to even ask them to do so..."

Children's menu.......................... ✓ $$.. Prices
Changing station .... ✓ ❹ ....Customer service
Highchairs/boosters..................... ✓ ❹ .... Stroller access

WWW.DUCLAW.COM

HANOVER—7000 ARUNDEL MILLS CIR (AT ARUNDEL MILL MALL); 410.799.1166; SU M 11-12, W-SA 11-2; MALL PARKING

Friendly's

"...we love Friendly's because it's fast, fun and the food is pretty good... you may wait a bit for your service, but given the promise of a sundae most kids will persevere... colorful menu and M&M pancakes... desert and a drink are included with some kids meals... convenient if you have kids of varying ages—there's something good for everyone... burgers, sandwiches and more fries than you'll know what to do with..."

Children's menu	✓	$$	Prices
Changing station	✓	❸	Customer service
Highchairs/boosters	✓	❸	Stroller access

WWW.FRIENDLYS.COM

CROFTON—1673 CROFTON CTR (AT CRAIN HWY); 410.721.3007; SU-TH 7-11, F-SA 7-12; FREE PARKING

EDGEWATER—112 MITCHELLS CHANCE RD (AT COLONY CLUB DR); 410.956.1732; SU-TH 7-11, F-SA 7-12; FREE PARKING

GLEN BURNIE—412 CRAIN HWY SW (AT 4TH AVE); 410.768.4910; SU-TH 7-11, F-SA 7-12

GLEN BURNIE—7134 RITCHIE HWY (AT E FURNACE BRANCH RD); 410.761.7362; SU-TH 7-11, F-SA 7-12; FREE PARKING

HANOVER—2641 JESSUP RD (AT BALTIMORE WASHINGTON PKY N); 410.551.0440; SU-TH 7-11, F-SA 7-12

PASADENA—4189 MOUNTAIN RD (AT MAGOTHY BEACH RD); 410.437.6085; SU-TH 7-11, F-SA 7-12

Fuddruckers

"...a super burger chain with fresh and tasty food... colorful and noisy with lots of distraction until the food arrives... loads of fresh toppings so that you can make your perfectly cooked burger even better... great kids deals that come with a free treat... noise not a problem in this super casual atmosphere... some locations have video games in the back which will buy you an extra half hour if you need it... low-key and very family friendly..."

Children's menu	✓	$$	Prices
Changing station	✓	❹	Customer service
Highchairs/boosters	✓	❹	Stroller access

WWW.FUDDRUCKERS.COM

ANNAPOLIS—175 JENNIFER RD (AT ANNAPOLIS MALL); 410.266.8030; M-TH 11-10, F-SA 11-10:30, SU 11-9

Johnny Rockets

"...burgers, fries and a shake served up in a 50's style diner... we love the singing waiters—they're always good for a giggle... my daughter is enthralled with the juke box and straw dispenser... sit at the counter and watch the cooks prepare the food... simple, satisfying and always a hit with the little ones..."

Children's menu	✓	$$	Prices
Changing station	×	❹	Customer service
Highchairs/boosters	✓	❸	Stroller access

WWW.JOHNNYROCKETS.COM

ANNAPOLIS—1084 ANNAPOLIS MALL (AT RESEARCH DR); 410.897.0717; M-TH 9-10, F-SA 9-11, SU 9-9; MALL PARKING

Red Robin

"...very kid-oriented—loud, balloons, bright lights, colorful decor and a cheerful staff make Red Robin a favorite among parents and children... the food is mainly burgers (beef or chicken)... loud music covers even the most boisterous of screaming... lots of kids—all the time... sometimes the wait can be long, but the arcade games and balloons help pass the time..."

Children's menu	✓	$$	Prices

Changing station .... ✓ ❹ ....Customer service
Highchairs/boosters .... ✓ ❹ .... Stroller access

WWW.REDROBIN.COM

ANNAPOLIS—1073 ANNAPOLIS MALL (AT JENNIFER RD); 410.573.1155; M-TH 11-10,, F-SA 11-11, SU 11-9; MALL PARKING

Romano's Macaroni Grill ★★★★★

"...family oriented and tasty... noisy so nobody cares if your kids make noise... the staff goes out of their way to make families feel welcome... they even provide slings by the table for infant carriers... the noise level is pretty constant so it's not too loud, but loud enough so that crying babies don't disturb the other patrons... good kids' menu with somewhat healthy items... crayons for kids to color on the paper tablecloths..."

Children's menu .... ✓ $$$ .... Prices
Changing station .... ✓ ❹ ....Customer service
Highchairs/boosters .... ✓ ❹ .... Stroller access

WWW.MACARONIGRILL.COM

ANNAPOLIS—178 JENNIFER RD (AT ANNAPOLIS MALL); 410.573.1717; SU-TH 11-10, F-SA 11-11; MALL PARKING

Ruby Tuesday ★★★½☆

"...nice variety of healthy choices on the kids' menu—turkey, spaghetti, chicken tenders... you can definitely find something healthy here... prices are on the high side, but at least everyone can find something they like... service is fast and efficient... my daughter makes a mess and they never let me clean it up... your typical chain, but it works—you'll be happy to see ample aisle space, storage for your stroller, and attentive staff..."

Children's menu .... ✓ $$ .... Prices
Changing station .... ✓ ❹ ....Customer service
Highchairs/boosters .... ✓ ❸ .... Stroller access

WWW.RUBYTUESDAY.COM

ANNAPOLIS—2025 SOMERVILLE RD (OFF RT 2); 410.266.7669; M-TH 11-11, F-SA 11-12, SU 11-10

GLEN BURNIE—7900 GOVERNOR RITCHIE HWY (AT MALEY STATION SHOPPING CTR); 410.766.4446; M-TH 11-11, F-SA 11-12, SU 11-10

Texas Roadhouse ★★★★★

"...loud enough to cover a crying baby... big booths to set your car seat in... we go to Texas Roadhouse on a monthly basis... we really enjoy the atmosphere and the friendly neighborhood feeling... great take home service too..."

Children's menu .... ✓ $$ .... Prices
Changing station .... ✓ ❹ ....Customer service
Highchairs/boosters .... ✓ ❸ .... Stroller access

WWW.TEXASROADHOUSE.COM

PASADENA—4465 MOUNTAIN RD (AT PENN DR); 410.439.0233; M-TH 4-10, F 4-11, SA 2-11, SU 12-10

TGI Friday's ★★★★☆

"...good old American bar food with a reasonable selection for the healthier set as well... I love that the kids meal includes salad... my daughter requests the potato skins on a regular basis (which is good because they are also my favorite)... moderately priced... cheerful servers are used to the mess my kids leave behind... relaxed scene... I'd steer clear on a Friday night unless you don't mind waiting and watching the singles scene..."

Children's menu .... ✓ $$ .... Prices
Changing station .... ✓ ❹ ....Customer service
Highchairs/boosters .... ✓ ❸ .... Stroller access

WWW.TGIFRIDAYS.COM

ANNAPOLIS—2582 SOLOMONS ISLAND RD (AT ARIES T ALLEN BLVD); 410.224.2839; DAILY 11:30-1:30

HANOVER—7655 ARUNDEL MILLS BLVD (AT ARUNDEL MILLS BLVD); 410.379.6762; DAILY 11-2

East of Baltimore

"lila picks"

★ Panera Bread

Don Pablo's

"...yummy Mexican dishes... spacious and super kid-friendly—we've been coming here since our baby was 2 weeks old... kid's meals are inexpensive and plentiful... my son loves playing with the dough and the meal arrives in no time... fun, boisterous setting... can get busy, but you generally get a table with little delay..."

Children's menu .... ✓ $$ .... Prices
Changing station .... ✓ ❹ .... Customer service
Highchairs/boosters .... ✓ ❹ .... Stroller access

WHITE MARSH—8161 HONEYGO BLVD (AT WHITE MARSH MAL); 410.931.7966; M-TH 11:30-10, F-SA 11:30-11

Friendly's

"...we love Friendly's because it's fast, fun and the food is pretty good... you may wait a bit for your service, but given the promise of a sundae most kids will persevere... colorful menu and M&M pancakes... desert and a drink are included with some kids meals... convenient if you have kids of varying ages—there's something good for everyone... burgers, sandwiches and more fries than you'll know what to do with..."

Children's menu .... ✓ $$ .... Prices
Changing station .... ✓ ❸ .... Customer service
Highchairs/boosters .... ✓ ❸ .... Stroller access

WWW.FRIENDLYS.COM

ESSEX—1101 EASTERN BLVD (AT GLENWOOD RD); 410.238.2015; SU-TH 7-11, F-SA 7-12

IKEA

"...Swedish meatballs and funny berry drinks—all very yummy and cheap... a clean, comfortable place to eat... the restaurant sells baby food and has bottle/jar warmers... worth visiting even if you aren't shopping—the food is cheap, but good... totally kid-friendly... lines can sometimes be long—especially during peak shopping hours..."

Children's menu .... ✓ $$ .... Prices
Changing station .... ✓ ❹ .... Customer service
Highchairs/boosters .... ✓ ❹ .... Stroller access

WWW.IKEA.COM

WHITE MARSH—8352 HONEYGO BLVD (AT WHITE MARSH BLVD); 410.931.5400; M-F 10-9, SA 9-9, SU 10-8

Olive Garden

"...finally a place that is both kid and adult friendly... tasty Italian chain with lots of convenient locations... the staff consistently attends to the details of dining with babies and toddlers—minimizing wait time,

highchairs offered spontaneously, bread sticks brought immediately... food is served as quickly as possible... happy to create special orders... our waitress even acted as our family photographer... ❞

Children's menu ✓ | $$ Prices
Changing station ✓ | ❹ Customer service
Highchairs/boosters ✓ | ❹ Stroller access

WWW.OLIVEGARDEN.COM

WHITE MARSH—8245 PERRY HALL BLVD (AT WHITE MARSH MALL); 410.931.3316; SU-TH 11-10, F-SA 11-11; MALL PARKING

Panera Bread

❝*...soups, sandwiches and delicious desserts... self-service food at great prices... the booths are big enough to put your car seat and store your stuff... fresh bread make their sandwiches special... some locations have a have a community room which is a great place for my moms group to sit, park our strollers and breast feed if need be...* ❞

Children's menu ✗ | $$ Prices
Changing station ✓ | ❹ Customer service
Highchairs/boosters ✓ | ❹ Stroller access

WWW.PANERABREAD.COM

ROSEDALE—8620 PULASKI HWY (OFF I-695); 410.238.0887; M-SA 6-9, SU 7-8

Ruby Tuesday

❝*...nice variety of healthy choices on the kids' menu—turkey, spaghetti, chicken tenders... you can definitely find something healthy here... prices are on the high side, but at least everyone can find something they like... service is fast and efficient... my daughter makes a mess and they never let me clean it up... your typical chain, but it works—you'll be happy to see ample aisle space, storage for your stroller, and attentive staff...* ❞

Children's menu ✓ | $$ Prices
Changing station ✓ | ❹ Customer service
Highchairs/boosters ✓ | ❸ Stroller access

WWW.RUBYTUESDAY.COM

WHITE MARSH—8200 PERRY HALL BLVD (AT WHITE MARSH MALL); 410.931.3278; M-TH 11-11, F-SA 11-12AM, SU 11-10

Strapazza of White Marsh

Children's menu ✗ | ✗ Changing station
Highchairs/boosters ✓

WWW.STRAPAZZA.COM

WHITE MARSH—8145 HONEYGO BLVD (AT WHITE MARSH MALL); 410.931.3177; SU-TH 11-10, F-SA 11-11

TGI Friday's

❝*...good old American bar food with a reasonable selection for the healthier set as well... I love that the kids meal includes salad... my daughter requests the potato skins on a regular basis (which is good because they are also my favorite)... moderately priced... cheerful servers are used to the mess my kids leave behind... relaxed scene... I'd steer clear on a Friday night unless you don't mind waiting and watching the singles scene...* ❞

Children's menu ✓ | $$ Prices
Changing station ✓ | ❹ Customer service
Highchairs/boosters ✓ | ❸ Stroller access

WWW.TGIFRIDAYS.COM

WHITE MARSH—4921 CAMPBELL BLVD (AT HONEYGO BLVD); 410.931.3090; DAILY 11-1

doulas & lactation consultants

Editor's Note: Doulas and lactation consultants provide a wide range of services and are very difficult to classify, let alone rate. In fact the terms 'doula' and 'lactation consultant' have very specific industry definitions that are far more complex than we are able to cover in this brief guide. For this reason we have decided to list only those businesses and individuals who received overwhelmingly positive reviews, without listing the reviewers' comments.

Greater Baltimore Area

ABC Doula Service

Labor doula .... ✓ ✓ .... Postpartum doula
Pre & post natal massage .... ✗ ✓ .... Lactation consultant

WWW.HOMESTEAD.COM/TWODOULAS/ABCDOULA.HTML

BALTIMORE—410.672.1477

Association of Labor Assistants & Childbirth Educators (ALACE)

Labor doula .... ✓ ✗ .... Postpartum doula
Pre & post natal massage .... ✗ ✗ .... Lactation consultant

WWW.ALACE.ORG

BALTIMORE—617.441.2500

Be Shaah Tovah (In Due Time)

Labor doula .... ✓ ✓ .... Postpartum doula
Pre & post natal massage .... ✗ ✓ .... Lactation consultant

WWW.BESHAAHTOVAH.COM

PIKESVILLE—410.653.7577

Chesapeake Birth Companions

Labor doula .... ✓ ✓ .... Postpartum doula
Pre & post natal massage .... ✗ ✓ .... Lactation consultant

WWW.CHESAPEAKEBIRTHCOMPANIONS.COM

BALTIMORE—443.254.3138

Doulas of North America (DONA)

Labor doula .... ✓ ✓ .... Postpartum doula
Pre & post natal massage .... ✗ ✗ .... Lactation consultant

WWW.DONA.ORG

BALTIMORE—888.788.3662

Greater Baltimore Medical Center (Lactation Station)

Labor doula .... ✗ ✗ .... Postpartum doula
Pre & post natal massage .... ✗ ✓ .... Lactation consultant

WWW.GBMC.ORG

TOWSON—6700 N CHARLES ST; 443.849.6262; CHECK SCHEDULE ONLINE; FREE PARKING

La Leche League

Labor doula .... ✗ ✗ .... Postpartum doula
Pre & post natal massage .... ✗ ✓ .... Lactation consultant

WWW.LALECHELEAGUE.ORG

BALTIMORE—VARIOUS LOCATIONS; 847.519.7730; CHECK SCHEDULE ONLINE; FREE PARKING

Special Beginnings

Labor doula .... ✓ ✓ .... Postpartum doula
Pre & post natal massage .... ✓ ✓ .... Lactation consultant

WWW.SPECIALBEGINNINGS.COM

ARNOLD—1454 BALTIMORE-ANNAPOLIS BLVD (OFF RITCHIE HWY); 410.626.8982

St Joseph Medical Center

Labor doula .... ✗ ✗ .... Postpartum doula
Pre & post natal massage .... ✗ ✓ .... Lactation consultant

WWW.SJMCMD.COM

TOWSON—7601 OSLER DR (AT STEVENSON LN); 410.337.3994; M-SA 7-4

exercise

Baltimore City

"lila picks"

★Dynamic Women

★Stroller Strides

Bally Total Fitness

"...whirlpool, child play center, personal trainers—this place really has it all... their day care makes it possible to have a great time working out and not worry about leaving your child behind... some locations have pools and spas too... lots of group classes so it's a nice way to meet new (postnatal) moms..."

Prenatal .... ✗ | $$$ .... Prices
Mommy & me .... ✗ | ❸ .... Decor
Child care available .... ✓ | ❸ .... Customer service

WWW.BALLYFITNESS.COM

BALTIMORE—2323 NORTHPOINT BLVD (OFF I-695); 410.282.2200; CHECK SCHEDULE ONLINE

Dynamic Women

"...beautiful, clean facilities that offer a variety of aerobics and fitness classes... a great, women-only gym that also offers childcare... my kids and I love coming here—I get to work out with my friends, and my son gets to play with his..."

Prenatal .... ✗ | $$$ .... Prices
Mommy & me .... ✗ | ❸ .... Decor
Child care available .... ✓ | ❸ .... Customer service

WWW.DYNAMICWOMEN.ORG

BALTIMORE—8649 PHILADELPHIA RD (AT ROTHVILLE BLVD); 410.780.5200; M-TH 9-8:30, F 9-6, SA 9-1 ; PARKING LOT

Meadow Mill Athletic Club

"...a bit pricey, but very nice amenities... what really makes this place so kid friendly is the 'Kids Room' for children 12 weeks to 12 years old... a separate nursery for infants, an arts and crafts center, tons of activities, and exercise programs for toddlers!.. very cute and artistic area with lots for the little ones to enjoy..."

Prenatal .... ✓ | $$$$$ .... Prices
Mommy & me .... ✗ | ❹ .... Decor
Child care available .... ✓ | ❹ .... Customer service

WWW.MEADOWMILL.COM

BALTIMORE—3600 CLIPPER MILL RD (OFF 41ST ST); 410.235.7000; M-TH 6-10, F 6-9 SA-SU 8-5PM; PARKING LOT

Midtown Yoga

"...affordable rates... clean and nice facility... variety of teachers who all have quite an individual style... some are more energetic, some are more calming... nice place with a very passionate staff..."

Prenatal ✓ | $$$ Prices
Mommy & me ✗ | ❸ Decor
Child care available ✗ | ❸ Customer service

WWW.MIDTOWNYOGA.ORG

BALTIMORE—107 E PRESTON ST (AT N CALVERT ST); 410.234.8967; CHECK SCHEDULE ONLINE

Quantum Yoga & Wellness

"...wonderful class techniques, and very personable staff... have a great kids camp for ages five to eight, and a family workshop for all ages..."

Prenatal ✓ | $$ Prices
Mommy & me ✓ | ❺ Decor
Child care available ✓ | ❸ Customer service

WWW.QUANTUMYOGA.COM

BALTIMORE—6080 FALLS RD (AT W LAKE AVE); 410.377.4800; CHECK SCHEDULE ONLINE

Stroller Strides

"...fantastic fun and very effective for losing those post-baby pounds... this is the greatest way to stay in shape as a mom—you have your baby in the stroller with you the whole time... the instructors are very professional, knowledgeable and motivating... beautiful, outdoor locations... classes consist of power walking combined with body toning exercises using exercise tubing and strollers... a great way to bond with my baby and other moms..."

Prenatal ✗ | $$ Prices
Mommy & me ✓ | ❹ Decor
Child care available ✗ | ❺ Customer service

WWW.STROLLERSTRIDES.NET

BALTIMORE—VARIOUS LOCATIONS; 800.829.0416; CHECK SCHEDULE ONLINE

exercise

Yama Studio

"...pre-natal yoga classes here were wonderfully relaxing, and helped me make it through some of the challenges of pregnancy..."

Prenatal ✗ | $ Prices
Mommy & me ✗ | ❺ Decor
Child care available ✗ | ❸ Customer service

WWW.YAMASTUDIO.COM

BALTIMORE—2654 MARYLAND AVE (AT W 26TH ST); 443.622.9642; CHECK SCHEDULE ONLINE

YMCA

"...the variety of fitness programs offered is astounding... class types and quality vary from facility to facility, but it's a must for new moms to check out... most facilities offer some kind of kids' activities or childcare so you can time your workouts around the classes... aerobics, yoga, pool—our Y even offers Pilates now... my favorite classes are the mom & baby yoga... the best bang for your buck... they have it all—great programs that meet the needs of a diverse range of families..."

Prenatal ✓ | $$$ Prices
Mommy & me ✓ | ❸ Decor
Child care available ✓ | ❸ Customer service

WWW.YMCAMD.ORG

BALTIMORE—1609 DRUID HILL AVE (AT MCMECHEN ST); 410.728.1600; M-F 6:30-10, SA 7-6, SU 12-5; FREE PARKING

North of Baltimore

"lila picks"

★Dynamic Women

Bally Total Fitness

"...whirlpool, child play center, personal trainers—this place really has it all... their day care makes it possible to have a great time working out and not worry about leaving your child behind... some locations have pools and spas too... lots of group classes so it's a nice way to meet new (postnatal) moms..."

Prenatal .... ✗ | $$$ .... Prices
Mommy & me .... ✗ | ❸ .... Decor
Child care available .... ✓ | ❸ .... Customer service

WWW.BALLYFITNESS.COM

TOWSON—1 E JOPPA RD; 410.337.0088; CHECK SCHEDULE ONLINE

Bel Air Athletic Club

"...great gym with excellent facilities and programs for children... cutting edge programming, exceptional facilities, and very supportive, helpful staff... super fancy and super pricey..."

Prenatal .... ✗ | $ .... Prices
Mommy & me .... ✗ | ❺ .... Decor
Child care available .... ✓ | ❸ .... Customer service

WWW.BAAC.COM

BEL AIR—658 BOULTON ST (AT HARFORD MALL); 410.838.2670; M-F 5:30-11 SA 7-7 SU 8-6; PARKING LOT

Dynamic Women

"...beautiful, clean facilities that offer a variety of aerobics and fitness classes... a great, women-only gym that also offers childcare... my kids and I love coming here—I get to work out with my friends, and my son gets to play with his..."

Prenatal .... ✗ | $$$ .... Prices
Mommy & me .... ✗ | ❸ .... Decor
Child care available .... ✓ | ❸ .... Customer service

WWW.DYNAMICWOMEN.ORG

TOWSON—929 TAYLOR AVE (AT LOCH RAVEN BLVD); 410.583.0929; CHECK SCHEDULE ONLINE

YMCA

"...the variety of fitness programs offered is astounding... class types and quality vary from facility to facility, but it's a must for new moms to check out... most facilities offer some kind of kids' activities or childcare so you can time your workouts around the classes... aerobics, yoga, pool—our Y even offers Pilates now... my favorite classes are the mom & baby yoga... the best bang for your buck... they have it all—great programs that meet the needs of a diverse range of families..."

Prenatal	✓	$$	Prices
Mommy & me	✓	❹	Decor
Child care available	✓	❸	Customer service

WWW.YMCAMD.ORG

TOWSON—600 W CHESAPEAKE AVE (AT DIXIE DR); 410.823.8870; M-F 5:30-10, SA 7-8, SU 8-8; FREE PARKING

YogaKids

"...awesome yoga program for kids and adults... love the mommy and baby class... a great way to get in shape while spending time with my daughter... when your baby starts crawling there is a toddler class available..."

Prenatal	✗	$$$	Prices
Mommy & me	✓	❸	Decor
Child care available	✗	❸	Customer service

GLEN ARM—12124 HOOPER LN (AT GLEN ARM RD E); 410.592.3242; CHECK SCHEDULE ONLINE

West of Baltimore

"lila picks"

★Dynamic Women

Avalon Studio (Movement & Dance)

"...Ann Israel conducts pre-natal and post-natal 'mommy and me' yoga classes, which are fantastic!.. she is also a lactation consultant and birthing instructor, and is incredibly warm, helpful,and knowledgeable... dance, tai chi, and other classes offered as well..."

Prenatal .... ✗ | $ .... Prices
Mommy & me .... ✗ | ❺ .... Decor
Child care available .... ✗ | ❸ .... Customer service

WWW.AVALONYOGASTUDIO.COM

CATONSVILLE—15 MELLOR AVE (AT MAGRUDER AVE); 410.869.9771; CHECK SCHEDULE ONLINE; PARKING LOT

Bally Total Fitness

★★★½☆

"...whirlpool, child play center, personal trainers—this place really has it all... their day care makes it possible to have a great time working out and not worry about leaving your child behind... some locations have pools and spas too... lots of group classes so it's a nice way to meet new (postnatal) moms..."

Prenatal .... ✗ | $$$ .... Prices
Mommy & me .... ✗ | ❸ .... Decor
Child care available .... ✓ | ❸ .... Customer service

WWW.BALLYFITNESS.COM

CATONSVILLE—6516 BALTIMORE PIKE (EAST OF N ROLLING RD); 410.744.8444; CHECK SCHEDULE ONLINE

Catonsville Jazzercise Fitness Center

Prenatal .... ✗ | ✗ .... Mommy & me
Child care available .... ✓

WWW.JAZZFIT.COM

CATONSVILLE—77 MELLOR AVE (OFF MAGRUDER AVE); 410.744.6800; M-TH 9-12 4:30-8, F 9-12, SA 8:30-12

Dynamic Women

"...beautiful, clean facilities that offer a variety of aerobics and fitness classes... a great, women-only gym that also offers childcare... my kids and I love coming here—I get to work out with my friends, and my son gets to play with his..."

Prenatal .... ✗ | $$$ .... Prices
Mommy & me .... ✗ | ❸ .... Decor
Child care available .... ✓ | ❸ .... Customer service

WWW.DYNAMICWOMEN.ORG

OWINGS MILLS—10300 REISTERSTOWN RD (OFF OWINGS MILLS BLVD); 410.902.6700; CHECK SCHEDULE ONLINE

Lynne Brick's Women's Health & Fitness

Prenatal .... ✗ ✓ .... Mommy & me
Child care available .... ✓

WWW.BRICKBODIES.COM

OWINGS MILLS—9950 REISTERSTOWN RD (AT RT 140); 410.363.4600; CHECK SCHEDULE ONLINE

Steller Fitness

"...this is a one on one slow burn experience... it's a great workout and it's quick... highly recommended..."

Prenatal .... ✗ $ .... Prices
Mommy & me .... ✗ ❺ .... Decor
Child care available .... ✗ ❸ .... Customer service

PIKESVILLE—1777 REISTERSTOWN RD (AT I-695); 410.602.2348; CHECK SCHEDULE ONLINE

YMCA

"...the variety of fitness programs offered is astounding... class types and quality vary from facility to facility, but it's a must for new moms to check out... most facilities offer some kind of kids' activities or childcare so you can time your workouts around the classes... aerobics, yoga, pool—our Y even offers Pilates now... my favorite classes are the mom & baby yoga... the best bang for your buck... they have it all—great programs that meet the needs of a diverse range of families..."

Prenatal .... ✓ $$$ .... Prices
Mommy & me .... ✓ ❸ .... Decor
Child care available .... ✓ ❸ .... Customer service

WWW.YMCAMD.ORG

CATONSVILLE—850 S ROLLING RD (AT CAMPUS DR); 410.747.9622; M-F 5:30-9:45, SA 7-6:45, SU 10-6:45; FREE PARKING

East of Baltimore

"lila picks"

★Dynamic Women

Dynamic Women

"...beautiful, clean facilities that offer a variety of aerobics and fitness classes... a great, women-only gym that also offers childcare... my kids and I love coming here—I get to work out with my friends, and my son gets to play with his..."

Prenatal	✗	$$$	Prices
Mommy & me	✗	❸	Decor
Child care available	✓	❸	Customer service

WWW.DYNAMICWOMEN.ORG

DUNDALK—7836 WISE AVE (OFF MERITT BLVD); 410.285.4111; CHECK SCHEDULE ONLINE

parent education & support

Baltimore City

"lila picks"

★Natural Approach To Parenting

ABC Doula Service

Childbirth classes .... ✗   ✓ .... Breastfeeding support
Parent group/club .... ✗   ✗ .... Child care info

WWW.HOMESTEAD.COM/TWODOULAS/ABCDOULA.HTML

BALTIMORE—410.672.1477

African-American Breastfeeding Alliance

Childbirth classes .... ✗   ✓ .... Breastfeeding support
Parent group/club .... ✓   ✓ .... Child care info

WWW.SJMCMD.COM

BALTIMORE—940 MADISON AVE (OFF CHASE ST); 410.225.2006

Alternative Birth Choices

Childbirth classes .... ✗   ✗ .... Breastfeeding support
Parent group/club .... ✗   ✗ .... Child care info

RANDALLSTOWN—5310 OLD COURT RD (AT LIBERTY RD); 410.521.2560

Bradley Method, The ★★★½☆

"...12 week classes that cover all of the basics of giving birth... run by individual instructors nationwide... classes differ based on the quality and experience of the instructor... they cover everything from nutrition and physical conditioning to spousal support and medication... wonderful series that can be very educational... their web site has listings of instructors on a regional basis..."

Childbirth classes .... ✓ $$$ .... Prices
Parent group/club .... ✗   ❸ .... Class selection
Breastfeeding support .... ✗   ❸ .... Staff knowledge
Child care info .... ✗   ❸ .... Customer service

WWW.BRADLEYBIRTH.COM

BALTIMORE—VARIOUS LOCATIONS; 800.422.4784; CHECK SCHEDULE & LOCATIONS ONLINE

Franklin Square Hospital Center

Childbirth classes .... ✗   ✗ .... Breastfeeding support
Parent group/club .... ✓   ✓ .... Child care info

WWW.FRANKLINSQUARE.ORG

BALTIMORE—9000 FRANKLIN SQ DR (AT ROSSVILLE BLVD); 443.777.7427

ICAN

"...a fantastic resource for those recovering from a C-Section... everything you need to know about cesareans is covered... meetings are free and open to the public..."

Childbirth classes	✓	$	Prices
Parent group/club	✓	❺	Class selection
Breastfeeding support	✓	❺	Staff knowledge
Child care info	×	❺	Customer service

WWW.ICAN-ONLINE.ORG

BALTIMORE—410.483.3202; 6:30PM 2ND TH OF EACH MONTH SEPT-MAY; CONTACT FOR DETAILS

Jewish Community Center

Childbirth classes	×	×	Breastfeeding support
Parent group/club	✓	✓	Child care info

WWW.PLANITJEWISH.COM

OWINGS MILLS—3506 GWYNNBROOK AVE (OFF GARRISON FOREST RD); 410.356.9342

Lamaze International

"...thousands of women each year are educated about the birth process by Lamaze educators... their web site offers a list of local instructors... they follow a basic curriculum, but invariably class quality will depend on the individual instructor... in many ways they've set the standard for birth education classes..."

Childbirth classes	✓	$$$	Prices
Parent group/club	×	❸	Class selection
Breastfeeding support	×	❸	Staff knowledge
Child care info	×	❸	Customer service

WWW.LAMAZE.ORG

BALTIMORE—VARIOUS LOCATIONS; 800.368.4404; CHECK SCHEDULE AND LOCATIONS ONLINE

Mocha Moms

"...a group geared toward stay at home moms of color... a wonderfully supportive group of women—the kind of place you'll make lifelong friends for both mother and child... a comfortable forum for bouncing ideas off of other moms with same-age children... easy to get involved and not too demanding... the annual membership dues seem a small price to pay for the many activities, play groups, field trips, Moms Nights Out and book club meetings... local chapters in cities nationwide..."

Childbirth classes	×	$$$	Prices
Parent group/club	✓	❸	Class selection
Breastfeeding support	×	❸	Staff knowledge
Child care info	×	❸	Customer service

WWW.MOCHAMOMS.ORG

BALTIMORE—VARIOUS LOCATIONS

MOMS Club

"...an international nonprofit with lots of local chapters and literally tens of thousands of members... designed to introduce you to new mothers with same-age kids wherever you live... they organize all sorts of activities and provide support for new mothers with babies... very inexpensive for all the activities you get... book clubs, moms night out, play group connections... generally a very diverse group of women..."

Childbirth classes	×	$$$	Prices
Parent group/club	✓	❸	Class selection
Breastfeeding support	×	❸	Staff knowledge
Child care info	×	❸	Customer service

WWW.MOMSCLUB.ORG
NORTH OF BALTIMORE—VARIOUS LOCATIONS
WEST OF BALTIMORE—VARIOUS LOCATIONS

Mothers and More

"...a very neat support system for moms who are deciding to stay at home... a great way to get together with other moms in your area for organized activities... book clubs, play groups, even a 'mom's only' night out... local chapters offer more or less activities depending on the involvement of local moms..."

Childbirth classes .... × | $$$ .... Prices
Parent group/club .... ✓ | ❸ .... Class selection
Breastfeeding support .... × | ❸ .... Staff knowledge
Child care info .... × | ❸ .... Customer service

WWW.MOTHERSANDMORE.COM
BALTIMORE—VARIOUS LOCATIONS; CHECK SCHEDULE & LOCATIONS ONLINE

Mothers Of Preschoolers (MOPS)

Childbirth classes .... × | × .... Breastfeeding support
Parent group/club .... ✓ | × .... Child care info

WWW.MOPS.ORG
LUTHERVILLE—1010 SATERS LN; 410.252.0409
REISTERSTOWN—1701 EMORY RD; 410.239.4700; W 7-9

Natural Approach To Parenting

"...a wonderful group where you can meet new parents and chat about the concerns, worries and joys of new parenthood... lots of guest speakers—they're usually pretty good... an easy way to find play groups... the focus is on organic and 'conscious' parenting—I like the vibe..."

Childbirth classes .... × | $$$ .... Prices
Parent group/club .... ✓ | ❸ .... Class selection
Breastfeeding support .... × | ❸ .... Staff knowledge
Child care info .... × | ❸ .... Customer service

WWW.TAKEANAP.ORG
BALTIMORE—VARIOUS LOCATIONS; 410.241.8757
BALTIMORE—VARIOUS LOCATIONS; 301.252.4843

Sinai Hospital

Childbirth classes .... × | ✓ .... Breastfeeding support
Parent group/club .... × | × .... Child care info

BALTIMORE—2435 W BELVEDERE AVE (AT GREENSPRING AVE); 410.601.5193

Special Beginnings

Childbirth classes .... × | ✓ .... Breastfeeding support
Parent group/club .... × | × .... Child care info

WWW.SPECIALBEGINNINGS.COM
ARNOLD—1454 BALTIMORE-ANNAPOLIS BLVD (OFF RITCHIE HWY); 410.626.8982

St Joseph Medical Center

Childbirth classes .... × | ✓ .... Breastfeeding support
Parent group/club .... × | × .... Child care info

WWW.SJMCMD.COM
TOWSON—7601 OSLER DR (AT STEVENSON LN); 410.337.3994; M-SA 7-4

pediatricians

Editor's Note: Pediatricians provide a tremendous breadth of services and are very difficult to classify and rate in a brief guide. For this reason we list only those practices for which we received overwhelmingly positive reviews. We hope this list of pediatricians will help you in your search.

Greater Baltimore Area

Andorsky, Michael MD

OWINGS MILLS—10085 RED RUN BLVD (AT PAINTERS MILL RD); 410.363.2240; M-TH 8:30-6:30, F 8:30-5, SA 8:30-11, SU 9-11

Cross Keys Pediatrics

BALTIMORE—2 HAMILL RD (AT CROSSKEYS RD); 410.323.1144; M W F 8:30-4:30, T TH 8:30-6, SA 9-12

Davidsonville Pediatrics

WWW.PEDIATRICGROUP.COM/DP.HTML

DAVIDSONVILLE—2772 RUTLAND RD (AT ST GEORGE BARBER RD); 410.798.1600; M-TH 7:30-7 F 7:30-5 SU 7:30-12

Hunt Manor Medical Associates

PHOENIX—3346 PAPER MILL RD (AT SWEET AIR RD); 410.666.4060; M-F 8:30-5; PARKING LOT

Joseph Berk MD

OWINGS MILLS—9199 REISTERSTOWN RD (AT MCDONOUGH RD); 410.654.4525; M-F 9-6, SA-SU 11-1; PARKING LOT

Main Street Pediatrics

TOWSON—515 FAIRMOUNT AVE (AT JOPPA RD); 410.494.1369; M-TH 8:30-6, F 8:30-5, SA-SU 9-12; GARAGE AT BLDG

Maryland Pediatric Group

WWW.MDPEDGRP.COM

LUTHERVILLE—10807 FALLS RD (AT W JOPPA RD); 410.321.9393; M-F 8:30-5

Wyman Park Medical Center Pediatrics

BALTIMORE—3100 WYMAN PARK DR (AT JOHN HOPKINS UNIVERSITY); 410.338.3071; M,TH 8-8 T,W,F 8-5 SA 9-1

breast pump sales & rentals

Greater Baltimore Area

"lila picks"

★Greater Baltimore Medical Center

A-1 Breastpumps, Nursing Bras, & More

WWW.A1BREASTPUMPS.COM

BALTIMORE—410.653.2023; FREE PARKING

Babies R Us

"...Medela pumps, Boppy pillows and lots of other breastfeeding supplies... staff knowledge varies from store to store, but everyone was friendly and helpful... clean and well-stocked... not a huge selection, but what they've got is great and very competitively priced..."

Customer Service .... ❹ $$$.. Prices

WWW.BABIESRUS.COM

CATONSVILLE—6501 BALTIMORE PIKE (AT N ROLLING RD); 410.744.0820; M-SA 9:30-9:30, SU 11-7; PARKING LOT

CATONSVILLE—6501A BALTIMORE NATL PIKE (AT 40 W PLZ); 410.744.0820; M-SA 9:30-9:30, SU 11-7 ; PARKING LOT

PASADENA—8100 RITCHIE HWY (AT JUNIPERS HOLE RD); 410.863.8840; M-SA 9:30-9:30, SU 11-7:30; PARKING IN FRONT OF BLDG

Greater Baltimore Medical Center (Lactation Station)

"...I have nothing, but good things to say about this store... a great idea... a little pricey, but very worth it, they have top of the line baby need items.. the lactation consultants here are always helpful and knowledgeable... the support group for new moms is an absolute must!..."

Customer Service .... ❺ $$$.. Prices

WWW.GBMC.ORG

TOWSON—6700 N CHARLES ST; 443.849.6262; CHECK SCHEDULE ONLINE; FREE PARKING

Mommies Milk

"...Kim at Mommies Milk is very helpful and flexible—she offers pumps, bras, slings, herbs and more... great storage rack, the oldest one is in the front so you use it first... I got my breastpump here—the price was great and I picked up my pump right away... the service was great and I got a great deal on my Ameda pump!..."

Customer Service .... ❸ $$$.. Prices

PARKVILLE—3334 WILLOUGHBY RD (AT AVONDALE RD); 410.663.4408

Right Start, The

"...a small selection of pumps for sale... their prices are on the higher side, and the pump selection is pretty limited... they carry the Medela

Pump In Style... they only carry the best... good quality and customer service might make it totally worthwhile... ”

Customer Service........................ ❸ $$$ .... Prices

WWW.RIGHTSTART.COM

ANNAPOLIS—1365 ANNAPOLIS MALL (AT ANNAPOLIS MALL); 410.571.9003; M-SA 10-9, SU 11-6; MALL PARKING

Special Beginnings

WWW.SPECIALBEGINNINGS.COM

ARNOLD—1454 BALTIMORE-ANNAPOLIS BLVD (OFF RITCHIE HWY); 410.626.8982

St Joseph Medical Center

WWW.SJMCMD.COM

TOWSON—7601 OSLER DR (AT STEVENSON LN); 410.337.3994; M-SA 7-4

Online

amazon.com

"...I'm always amazed by the amount of stuff Amazon sells—including a pretty good selection of pumps... Medela, Avent, Isis, Ameda... prices range from great to average... pretty easy shopping experience... free shipping on bigger orders..."

babycenter.com

"...they carry all the major brands... prices are competitive, but keep in mind you'll need to pay for shipping too... the comments from parents are incredibly helpful... excellent customer service... easy shopping experience..."

birthexperience.com

"...Medela and Avent products... great deal with the Canadian currency conversion... get free shipping with big orders... easy site to navigate..."

breast-pumps.com

breastmilk.com

ebay.com

"...you can get Medela pumps brand new in packaging with the warranty for $100 less than retail... able to buy immediately instead of having to bid and wait... wide variety... be sure to check for shipping price... great place to find deals, but research the seller before you bid..."

express-yourself.net

healthchecksystems.com

lactationconnection.com

"...Ameda and Whisper Wear products... nice selection and competitive prices... quick delivery of any nursing or lactation product you can imagine... the selection of mom and baby related items is fantastic..."

medela.com

"...well worth the money... fast, courteous and responsive... great site for a full listing of Medela products and links to purchase online... quality of customer service by phone varies... licensed lactation specialist answers e-mail via email at no charge and with quick turnaround..."

mybreastpump.com

"...a great online one-stop-shop for all things breast feeding... you can purchase hospital grade pumps from them... fast service for all you breastfeeding needs..."

diaper delivery services

Greater Baltimore Area

Modern Diaper Service

"...affordable and comfy diapers delivered to you door and pick up the dirties... made our lives easier and saved a whole lotta landfill space... reasonable prices and great customer service... I used them for five years!... reliable, flexible and generally prompt... able to cancel pickups or drop-offs at the last minute... pleasant drivers and office staff... certainly made cloth diapering easy..."

Customer Service .... ❸ $$$.. Prices

Service Area ... Greater Baltimore area

BALTIMORE—5318 EISENHOWER AVE; 301.853.3993

haircuts

Greater Baltimore Area

"lila picks"

★Cartoon Cuts

Cartoon Cuts

"...if your tot squirms at the thought of getting his hair cut, then you might want to try Cartoon Cuts... cartoons and toys catch your kid's attention while the cutters do their job... the staff is patient and friendly... cuts vary depending on the staff, so once you've found someone good I'd suggest coming back to her... lollipops are an extra added bonus... a fun waiting area and TV's at each station to keep the little ones happy... kids seem to love it..."

Customer Service .... ❺ $$.. Prices

WWW.CARTOONCUTS.COM

BALTIMORE—8200 PERRY HALL BLVD (AT LAKEFOREST MALL); 410.931.1588; MALL PARKING

BEL AIR—696-A BEL AIR RD (AT HARFORD MALL); 410.399.2104; M-F 10-9:30, SA 9-9:30, SU 11-5; MALL PARKING

GLEN BURNIE—7900 RITCHIE HWY (AT MARLEY STATION SHOPPING CTR); 410.768.9606; M-SA 10-9:30, SU 11-6; MALL PARKING

Hair Cuttery

"...if your tot squirms at the thought of getting his hair cut, then you might want to try Cartoon Cuts... cartoons and toys catch your kid's attention while the cutters do their job... the staff is patient and friendly... cuts vary depending on the staff, so once you've found someone good I'd suggest coming back to her... lollipops are an extra added bonus... a fun waiting area and TV's at each station to keep the little ones happy... kids seem to love it..."

Customer Service .... ❸ $$.. Prices

WWW.HAIRCUTTERY.COM

BALTIMORE—825 DULANEY VALLEY RD (AT TOWSON TWN CTR); 410.337.9841; MALL PARKING

REISTERSTOWN—11714-H REISTERSTOWN RD (AT CHESTNUT HILL LN); 410.833.9770; M-F 9-9, SA 9-8, SU 9-5

Head To Toes

"...owned by a parent who 'gets it'... fast service, kid friendly, a painless experience!..."

Customer Service .... ❺ $$.. Prices

WWW.HEADTOTOESSALON.COM

FOXBOROUGH—11 MECHANIC ST (AT COCASSET ST); 508.543.1112; M-W 9-8, TH 12-8, F 9-7, SA 9-3

nanny & babysitter referrals

Greater Baltimore Area

"lila picks"

★A Choice Nanny

★Nannies Inc

A Choice Nanny

"...they were very professional and knowledgeable about their nannies... we found a wonderful nanny in less than a month... the process was pretty painless and they really delivered... this service was very welcoming and I was sent on lots of interviews before I found the right fit..."

Baby nurses	×	$$$	Prices
Nannies	✓	❸	Candidate selection
Au pairs	×	❸	Staff knowledge
Babysitters	×	❸	Customer service
Service Area	Baltimore		

WWW.ACHOICENANNY.COM/BALTIMORE

TIMONIUM—201 W PADONIA RD (AT YORK RD); 410.823.8687; M-F 9-4

Nannies Inc

"...they specialize in long-term, professional nanny placement... nannies with at least 3 years of experience... it really is pretty simple and quick... their database is huge and they managed to present us with a bunch of candidates within days... courteous staff..."

Baby nurses	×	$$$	Prices
Nannies	✓	❸	Candidate selection
Au pairs	×	❸	Staff knowledge
Babysitters	×	❸	Customer service
Service Area	Baltimore & DC areas		

WWW.NANNIESINC.NET

ANNAPOLIS—410.267.0610; 24 HOURS

Nanny Network

"...they were quick and very efficient... I especially liked that you don't pay any fees unless they are successful at finding you a good match... they were really good at listening to my needs and trying to find good candidates for us... a great experience, through and through..."

Baby nurses	×	$$$	Prices
Nannies	✓	❸	Candidate selection
Au pairs	×	❸	Staff knowledge
Babysitters	×	❸	Customer service
Service Area	Baltimore metro area		

WWW.MDNANNY.COM

BALTIMORE—521 E JOPPA RD (AT PROVIDENCE RD); 410.321.1566; CALL FOR APPT

Online

"lila picks"

★craigslist.org

4nannies.com

Baby nurses .... ✗ ✓ .... Nannies
Au pairs .... ✗ ✗ .... Babysitters
Service Area .... nationwide
WWW.4NANNIES.COM

aupaircare.com

Baby nurses .... ✗ ✗ .... Nannies
Au pairs .... ✓ ✗ .... Babysitters
Service Area .... International
WWW.AUPAIRCARE.COM

aupairinamerica.com

Baby nurses .... ✗ ✗ .... Nannies
Au pairs .... ✓ ✗ .... Babysitters
Service Area .... International
WWW.AUPAIRINAMERICA.COM

babysitters.com

Baby nurses .... ✗ ✗ .... Nannies
Au pairs .... ✗ ✓ .... Babysitters
Service Area .... nationwide
WWW.BABYSITTERS.COM

craigslist.org ★★★★★

"...you can find just about anything on craigslist... good starting point, especially if you don't want to spend a lot of money and are willing to do your own screening... we received at least 50 responses to our 'nanny wanted' ad... helped me find very qualified baby-sitters... includes all major cities in the US..."

Baby nurses .... ✓ ✓ .... Nannies
Au pairs .... ✗ ✓ .... Babysitters
WWW.CRAIGSLIST.ORG

enannysource.com

Baby nurses .... ✗ ✓ .... Nannies
Au pairs .... ✗ ✗ .... Babysitters
Service Area .... nationwide
WWW.ENANNYSOURCE.COM

findcarenow.com

Baby nurses .... ✗ ✗ .... Nannies
Au pairs .... ✗ ✓ .... Babysitters
Service Area .... nationwide
WWW.FINDCARENOW.COM

get-a-sitter.com

Baby nurses .... ✗ ✗ .... Nannies
Au pairs .... ✗ ✓ .... Babysitters
Service Area ....nationwide
WWW.GET-A-SITTER.COM

householdstaffing.com

Baby nurses .... ✓ ✓ .... Nannies
Au pairs .... ✗ ✗ .... Babysitters
WWW.HOUSEHOLDSTAFFING.COM

interexchange.org

Baby nurses .... ✗ ✗ .... Nannies
Au pairs .... ✓ ✗ .... Babysitters
Service Area .... International
WWW.INTEREXCHANGE.ORG

nannies4hire.com

Baby nurses .... ✗ ✓ .... Nannies
Au pairs .... ✗ ✗ .... Babysitters
WWW.NANNIES4HIRE.COM

nannylocators.com ★★★☆☆

"...many listings of local nannies available... I have found that the listings are not always up to date... $100 subscriber fee to respond and contact nannies that have posted... different regions have varying amounts of listings available..."

Baby nurses .... ✗ ✓ .... Nannies
Au pairs .... ✗ ✗ .... Babysitters
Service Area .... Nationwide
WWW.NANNYLOCATORS.COM

sittercity.com ★★★★☆

"...wonderful online resource... an online baby-sitter database filled with mostly college and graduate students looking for baby-sitting and nanny jobs... candidates are not prescreened so you must check references... Fee to access the database is $35 plus $5 per month... tends to be be more useful for baby-sitters than regular daytime nannies..."

Baby nurses .... ✗ ✗ .... Nannies
Au pairs .... ✗ ✓ .... Babysitters
Service Area ....nationwide
WWW.SITTERCITY.COM

student-sitters.com

Baby nurses .... ✗ ✗ .... Nannies
Au pairs .... ✗ ✓ .... Babysitters
WWW.STUDENT-SITTERS.COM

photographers

Greater Baltimore Area

"lila picks"

★Bellies and Births

A Place In Time Photographic Designs

"...they do everything from weddings to babies... very courteous and professional... much better than the photos you get at the mall—these guys know what they're doing... gorgeous color and classic black and white..."

Customer service........................❸ $$$......................................Prices

WWW.APLACEINTIME.COM

BEL AIR—551 ROCK SPRING RD (AT DALLAM AVE); 410.879.0752

Bellies & Births

"...this is where science and art converge—Karen is so good at what she does... breathtaking images of my baby being born... I'm stunned every time I look at the album of my son's birth... she's a pleasure to work with..."

Customer service........................❸ $$$......................................Prices

Service Area ...Greater Baltimore area

WWW.BELLIESANDBIRTHS.COM

BALTIMORE—410.788.5605; CALL FOR APPT

Don Eisenhart Photography

Service Area .. Arundel Mills Mall area

WWW.DONEISENHART.COM

HANOVER—1515 DAVID VICTORIA LANES (AT HARMANS RD); 888.242.5651; CALL FOR APPT; PARKING AVAILABLE

JCPenney Portrait Studio

"...don't expect works of art, but they are great for a quick wallet photo... photographers and staff range from great to not so good... a quick portrait with standard props and backdrops... definitely join the portrait club and use coupons... waits are especially long around the holidays, so consider taking your Christmas pictures early... the e-picture option is a time saver... wait time for prints can be up to a month... look for coupons and you'll never have to pay full price..."

Customer service........................❹ $$..Prices

WWW.JCPENNEYPORTRAITS.COM

OWINGS MILLS—10400 MILL RUN CIR (AT OWINGS MILLS TOWN CTR); 410.654.4660

Picture People

"...this well-known photography chain offers good package deals that get even better with coupons... generally friendly staff despite the often 'uncooperative' little customers... they don't produce super fancy, artistic shots, but you get your pictures in under an hour... reasonable

quality for a fast portrait... kind of hit-or-miss quality and customer service... ❞

Customer service .... ❹ $$$ .... Prices

WWW.PICTUREPEOPLE.COM

ANNAPOLIS—21 ANNAPOLIS MALL (AT JENNIFER RD); 410.573.2932; MALL PARKING

GLEN BURNIE—7900 RITCHIE HWY (AT MARLEY STATION SHOPPING CTR); 410.590.4900; M-SA 10-9:30, SU 11-6

HANOVER—7000 ARUNDEL MILLS CIR (AT ARUNDEL MILLS BLVD); 410.799.0902; MALL PARKING

OWINGS MILLS—10300 MILL RUN CIR (AT OWINGS MILLS TOWN CTR); 410.363.9028

TOWSON—825 DULANEY VALLEY RD (AT TOWNSON TOWN CTR); 410.825.6135

WHITE MARSH—8200 PERRY HALL BLVD (AT HONEYGO BLVD); 410.931.9301

Richard Veytsman Photography ★★★★☆

❝*...very creative and prices are excellent... he's really professional and a pleasure to work with... he managed to coax the most wonderful expressions out of our daughter... priceless... packages are in the $100-$200 range depending on how many reprints you need...* ❞

Customer service .... ❺ $$ .... Prices

Service AreaGreater Baltimore and DC areas

WWW.RICHARDVEYTSMANPHOTOGRAPHY.COM

REISTERSTOWN—410.591.2999

Sears Portrait Studio ★★★☆☆

❝*...the price is right, but the service and quality are variable... make an appointment to cut down on the wait time... bring your coupons for even better prices... perfect for getting a nice wallet size portrait without spending a fortune... I wish the wait time for prints wasn't so long (2 weeks)... the quality and service-orientation of the photographers really vary a lot—some are great, some aren't...* ❞

Customer service .... ❸ $$ .... Prices

WWW.SEARSPORTRAIT.COM

ANNAPOLIS—1040 ANNAPOLIS MALL (AT JENNIFER RD); 410.573.5818; M-F 9:30-8 SA 9-8 SU 10-6; PARKING LOT

BALTIMORE—6901 SECURITY BLVD (AT SECURITY SQ MALL); 410.265.5758; MALL PARKING

BALTIMORE—7839 EASTPOINT MALL (AT NORTH POINT BLVD); 410.282.3496

BALTIMORE—8200 PERRY HALL BLVD (AT WHITE MARSH MALL); 410.931.0442

BEL AIR—658 BEL AIR RD (AT HARTFORD MALL); 410.420.1372

COCKEYSVILLE—126 SHAWAN RD (AT HUNT VALLEY MALL); 410.771.1847

GLEN BURNIE—7900 RITCHIE HWY (AT MARLEY STATION SHOPPING CTR); 410.863.0788

Online

clubphoto.com

WWW.CLUBPHOTO.COM

dotphoto.com

WWW.DOTPHOTO.COM

flickr.com

WWW.FLICKR.COM

kodakgallery.com

“...the popular ofoto.com is now under it's wings... very easy to use desktop software to upload your pictures on their site... prints, books, mugs and other photo gifts are reasonably priced and are always shipped promptly... I like that there is no limit to how many pictures and albums you can have their site...”

WWW.KODAKGALLERY.COM

photoworks.com

WWW.PHOTOWORKS.COM

shutterfly.com

“...I've spent hundreds of dollars with them—it's so easy and the quality of the pictures is great... they use really nice quality photo paper... what a lifesaver—since I store all of my pictures with them I didn't lose any when my computer crashed... most special occasions are take care of with a personal photo calendar, book or other item with the cutest pictures of our kids... reasonable prices...”

WWW.SHUTTERFLY.COM

snapfish.com

“...great photo quality and never a problem with storage limits... we love their photo books and flip books—easy to make and fun to give... good service and a good price... we have family that lives all over the country and yet everyone still gets to see and order pictures of our new baby...”

WWW.SNAPFISH.COM

indexes

alphabetical

by city/neighborhood

alphabetical

by city/neighborhood

Bel Air

Catonsville

Cockeysville

Crofton

Davidsonville

Notes

YOUR RECOMMENDATIONS MAKE THE LILAGUIDE BETTER!

PLEASE SHARE YOUR NOTES WITH US AT WWW.LILAGUIDE.COM

Notes

YOUR RECOMMENDATIONS MAKE THE LILAGUIDE BETTER!

PLEASE SHARE YOUR NOTES WITH US AT WWW.LILAGUIDE.COM

Notes

YOUR RECOMMENDATIONS MAKE THE LILAGUIDE BETTER!

PLEASE SHARE YOUR NOTES WITH US AT WWW.LILAGUIDE.COM

Notes

YOUR RECOMMENDATIONS MAKE THE LILAGUIDE BETTER!

PLEASE SHARE YOUR NOTES WITH US AT WWW.LILAGUIDE.COM

Notes

YOUR RECOMMENDATIONS MAKE THE LILAGUIDE BETTER!

PLEASE SHARE YOUR NOTES WITH US AT WWW.LILAGUIDE.COM

Notes

YOUR RECOMMENDATIONS MAKE THE LILAGUIDE BETTER!

PLEASE SHARE YOUR NOTES WITH US AT WWW.LILAGUIDE.COM

Notes

YOUR RECOMMENDATIONS MAKE THE LILAGUIDE BETTER!

PLEASE SHARE YOUR NOTES WITH US AT WWW.LILAGUIDE.COM

Notes

YOUR RECOMMENDATIONS MAKE THE LILAGUIDE BETTER!

PLEASE SHARE YOUR NOTES WITH US AT WWW.LILAGUIDE.COM

Notes

YOUR RECOMMENDATIONS MAKE THE LILAGUIDE BETTER!

PLEASE SHARE YOUR NOTES WITH US AT WWW.LILAGUIDE.COM

Notes

YOUR RECOMMENDATIONS MAKE THE LILAGUIDE BETTER!

PLEASE SHARE YOUR NOTES WITH US AT WWW.LILAGUIDE.COM

Notes

YOUR RECOMMENDATIONS MAKE THE LILAGUIDE BETTER!

PLEASE SHARE YOUR NOTES WITH US AT WWW.LILAGUIDE.COM

Notes

YOUR RECOMMENDATIONS MAKE THE LILAGUIDE BETTER!

PLEASE SHARE YOUR NOTES WITH US AT WWW.LILAGUIDE.COM

Notes

YOUR RECOMMENDATIONS MAKE THE LILAGUIDE BETTER!

PLEASE SHARE YOUR NOTES WITH US AT WWW.LILAGUIDE.COM

Notes

YOUR RECOMMENDATIONS MAKE THE LILAGUIDE BETTER!

PLEASE SHARE YOUR NOTES WITH US AT WWW.LILAGUIDE.COM

Notes

YOUR RECOMMENDATIONS MAKE THE LILAGUIDE BETTER!

PLEASE SHARE YOUR NOTES WITH US AT WWW.LILAGUIDE.COM

Notes

YOUR RECOMMENDATIONS MAKE THE LILAGUIDE BETTER!

PLEASE SHARE YOUR NOTES WITH US AT WWW.LILAGUIDE.COM

Notes

YOUR RECOMMENDATIONS MAKE THE LILAGUIDE BETTER!

PLEASE SHARE YOUR NOTES WITH US AT WWW.LILAGUIDE.COM

Notes

YOUR RECOMMENDATIONS MAKE THE LILAGUIDE BETTER!
PLEASE SHARE YOUR NOTES WITH US AT WWW.LILAGUIDE.COM